Management Accounting (MA)

Diploma in accounting and business

Pocket Notes

British library cataloguing-in-publication data

A catalogue record for this book is available from the British Library.

Published by:
Kaplan Publishing UK
Unit 2 The Business Centre
Molly Millars Lane
Wokingham
Berkshire
RG41 2QZ

ISBN 978-1-78740-471-7

Printed and bound in Great Britain.

Contents

Chapter 1 Accounting for management 1

Chapter 2 Sources of data and analysing data 9

Chapter 3 Presenting information 23

Chapter 4 Cost classification 29

Chapter 5 Accounting for materials 39

Chapter 6 Accounting for labour 49

Chapter 7 Accounting for overheads 57

Chapter 8 Absorption and marginal costing 67

Chapter 9 Job, batch and process costing 73

Chapter 10 Service and operation costing 93

Chapter 11 Alternative costing principles 97

Chapter 12 Statistical techniques 103

Chapter 13 Budgeting 109

Chapter 14 Capital budgeting 131

Chapter 15 Standard costing 143

Chapter 16   Performance measurement techniques 157

Chapter 17   Spreadsheets 167

Index I.1

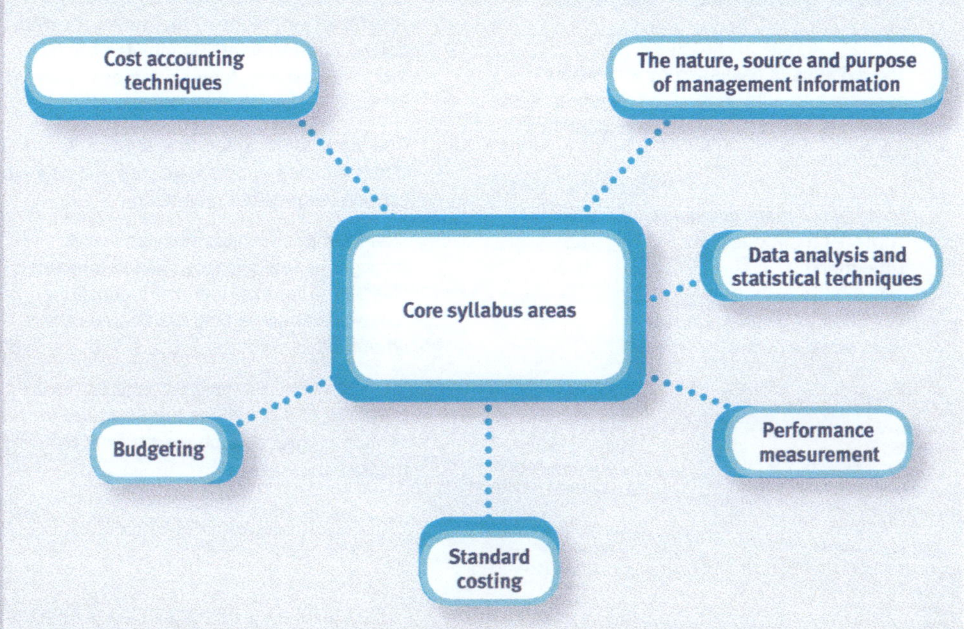

Cost accounting techniques
The nature, source and purpose of management information
Core syllabus areas
Data analysis and statistical techniques
Budgeting
Performance measurement
Standard costing

Exam guidance – keys to success in this paper

The syllabus is assessed by a two-hour paper or computer-based examination. Some questions will involve calculations, others will not.

	Number of marks
Thirty five 2-mark questions	70
Three 10-mark questions	30
Total marks	100

Total time allowed – 2 hours
Pass mark – 50%

Divide the time you spend on questions roughly in proportion to the marks allowed. Spend approximately 84 minutes on the 2-mark questions, leaving approximately 36 minutes for the 10-mark questions.

The exam is designed to test your understanding of principles, not just whether you can regurgitate information.

Read the question carefully and work through any calculations. Watch for words like "not" – for example some questions ask whether something is true and others whether it is not true.

Work steadily. Rushing leads to careless mistakes and questions are designed to include answers which results from careless mistakes.

Computer-based exam tips

Make sure you understand the software before you start. If in doubt ask the assessment centre staff to explain it. You can try a CBE Demo if you visit the Exam Support section of the ACCA's website.

Don't panic if you realise you have answered a question incorrectly. Getting one question wrong will not mean the difference between passing and failing.

You will receive your results immediately at the end of the exam.

You can take a CBE at any time in the year – you do not have to wait until the June or December exam sitting.

Linear regression

$$r = \frac{n\sum xy - \sum x \sum y}{\sqrt{[n\sum x^2 - (\sum x)^2][n\sum y^2 - (\sum y)^2]}}$$

If $y = a + bx$,

$$b = \frac{n\sum xy - \sum x \sum y}{n\sum x^2 - (\sum x)^2} \quad \text{and} \quad a = \frac{\sum y}{n} - b\frac{\sum x}{n}$$

Economic order quantity

$$\text{Economic order quantity} = \sqrt{\frac{2C_0 D}{C_H}}$$

$$\text{Economic batch quantity} = \sqrt{\frac{2C_0 D}{C_H\left(1 - \dfrac{D}{R}\right)}}$$

Arithmic mean

$$\bar{x} = \frac{\Sigma x}{n} \qquad \bar{x} = \frac{\Sigma fx}{\Sigma f} \text{ (frequency distribution)}$$

Standard deviation

$$\sigma = \sqrt{\frac{\Sigma(x - \bar{x})^2}{n}} \qquad \sigma = \sqrt{\frac{\Sigma fx^2}{\Sigma f} - \left(\frac{\Sigma fx}{\Sigma f}\right)^2}$$

(frequency distribution)

Variance $= \sigma^2$

Co-efficient of variaion $CV = \dfrac{\sigma}{\bar{x}}$

Expected value $EV = \Sigma px$

Quality and accuracy are of the utmost importance to us so if you spot an error in any of our products, please send an email to mykaplanreporting@kaplan.com with full details, or follow the link to the feedback form in MyKaplan.

Our Quality Co-ordinator will work with our technical team to verify the error and take action to ensure it is corrected in future editions.

Accounting for Management

In this chapter

- Data and information.
- Planning, decision making and control.
- Mission statement.
- Levels of planning.
- Responsibility centres.
- The role of management accounting.

Exam focus

It is important that you understand the information needs of managers, and in particular the different types of responsibility centres.

Data and information

Definition

Data and information are different.

- Data consists of numbers, letters, symbols, raw facts, events and transactions which have been recorded but not yet processed into a form suitable for use.

- Information is data which has been processed in such a way that it is meaningful to the person who receives it (for making decisions).

Key Point

Attributes of good information:

The 'ACCURATE' acronym:

- A – Accurate
- C – Complete
- C – Cost-effective
- U – Understandable
- R – Relevant
- A – Authoritative
- T – Timely
- E – Easy-to-use!

Planning, decision making and control

The main functions of management are planning, decision making and control.

The process	What is it?	Information needs
Planning	• First part of the decision making process • Establishing objectives and formulating strategies to achieve objectives short-term (tactical) or long-term	• What has happened in the past • What might happen in the future
Decision making	• Considering information provided and making an informed decision • Choosing between alternatives	• Reliable information on different courses of action • The consequences of different options
Control	• The second part of the decision making process • Comparing information on actual and planned results to take control measures and amend plans	• Information on actual results • Plans or targets • Internally-produced feedback

Mission statement

The mission statement is a statement in writing that describes the overall aims of an organisation.

There are four main elements:

- Purpose
- Strategy
- Policies and culture
- Values

Levels of Planning

Strategic, tactical and operational planning

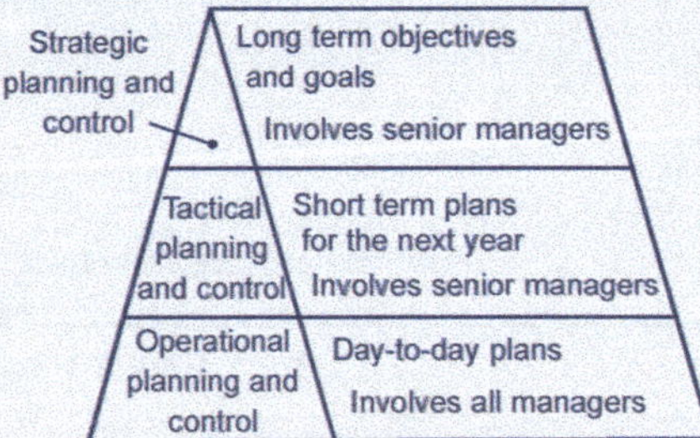

Responsibility centres

> **Definition**

A responsibility centre is an individual part of a business whose manager has personal responsibility for its performance. The main responsibility centres are:

- cost centre
- profit centre
- investment centre
- revenue centre.

Managers must be able to plan and control the areas of performance on which they are measured.

	Cost centre	Profit centre	Investment centre	Revenue centre
What is it?	Part of the business for which costs are identified and recorded	Part of the business for which costs incurred and revenue earned are identified and recorded	A part of the business for which profits and capital employed are measured	A part of the business for which revenues earned are identified and recorded
Where might it be found?	Any production or service location, function, activity, item of equipment	Divisions of large organisations. May include several cost and revenue centres	Business units of large organisations	Sales divisions
How is performance measured?	Have cost targets been achieved?	What profit has been made by the centre?	Return on capital employed	What revenue has been earned?
What are the manager's information needs?	Costs incurred and charged to cost centre	Information about costs and revenues allocated to the profit centre	Information on costs, revenues and capital employed by the investment centre	Sales revenue earned by the individual revenue centre

	Cost centre	Profit centre	Investment centre	Revenue centre
Example	Audit, tax, accountancy departments in an accounting firm	Wholesale and retail divisions in a paint company	UK and European divisions of a multinational company	Regional sales areas within the retail division of a manufacturing company

chapter 1

The role of management accounting

- Financial accounting: recording financial transactions and summarising them in periodic statements for external users.

- Cost accounting: recording data and producing information about the costs of products, activities and responsibility centres.

- Management accounting: provision of information about historical and future costs of products and services, providing financial and non-financial information to managers.

	Management accounting	Financial accounting
Information mainly produced for	Internal use: e.g. managers and employees	External use: e.g. shareholders, payables, lenders, banks, government
Purpose of information	To aid planning, control and decision making	To record the financial performance in a period and the financial position at the end of that period.
Legal requirements	None	Limited companies must produce financial accounts.
Formats	Management decide on the information they require and the most useful way of presenting it	Limited companies must produce financial accounts.

	Management accounting	Financial accounting
Nature of information	Financial and non-financial	Mostly financial
Time period	Historical and forward-looking	Mainly an historical record

Sources of data and analysing data

In this chapter

- Types of data.
- Internal sources of information.
- External sources of information.
- Sampling techniques.
- Big data.
- Averaging data and measures of spread.
- Averaging data example.
- Measures of spread example.
- Expected values and probability.
- Risk and uncertainty.
- Normal distribution.

It is important that you understand where information can be sourced from. It is also important to be able to identify which sampling technique would be most appropriate when.

Types of data

Primary data is data that is obtained directly from first-hand sources by means of surveys, observation or experimentation. It is data that has not been previously published. Primary data is any data which is used solely for the purpose for which it was originally collected.

Secondary data is any information that has been collected or researched recently. Sources of secondary data include the internet, libraries, company reports, newspaper, governments and banks. The data collected is useful as it allows the researcher to see the other opinions on their area of study but care must be taken that the data is reliable and accurate. Secondary data is data that has already been collected for some other purpose but can also be used for the purpose in hand.

Internal sources of information

- Accounting system
- Payroll system
- Planning system

Benefits

- Readily available
- Easy to sort and analyse
- Relates to the organisation concerned

Limitations

- May need further processing to be of use.

External sources of information

- Government
- Other businesses
- Trade associations
- Financial and business press
- Internet

Benefits

- Wide expanse
- Easily accessible
- General and specific information available

Limitations

- Accuracy
- Time consuming searches

Sampling techniques

Random sampling

A sample is taken in such a way that every member of the population has an equal chance of being selected.

Systematic sampling

The sample is taken by choosing a random initial number and then picking the nth item after that i.e. the first item is chosen as number 12, the next will be 112, then 212, then 312. The frequency of the nth item will depend on how big the sample population is and how many pieces of information are required.

Stratified sampling

The population is split into well defined groups (men and women, age groups etc) then a random sample is taken from each group.

Multi-stage sampling

Used if a population is very large – for example if a sample was required from a whole country (i.e. during a government election) the process would be:

1   The country is divided into areas and random sample is taken

2   Each sampled area (from 1) is divided into towns/cities and a random sample is taken

3   Each town/city (from 2) is divided into roads and a random sample is taken

4   From each road (from 3) random houses are sampled and the occupants questioned

Cluster sampling

Similar to multi-stage sampling but once the desired number of areas are chosen every occupant in that area would be part of the sample.

Quota sampling

The interviewer knows how many 'types' need to be interviewed i.e. 20 males between 20 and 29 years old. The interviewer will use any method to reach the sample size.

Big data

Definition

Extremely large collections of data that may be analysed to reveal patterns, trends and associations.

The processing of Big Data is known as Big Data analytics, for example using Hadoop software.

Characterised by the 3Vs

Volume — Organisations now hold huge volumes of data, for example on customer purchases.

Variety — Data can be financial or non-financial, internal or external, structured or unstructured.

Velocity — The data needs to be turned into useful information quickly.

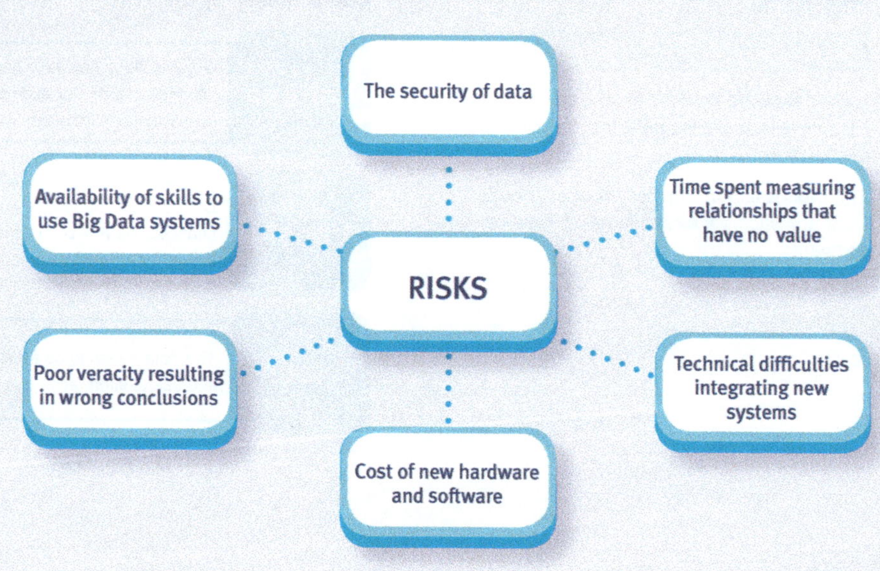

The security of data
Availability of skills to use Big Data systems
Time spent measuring relationships that have no value
RISKS
Poor veracity resulting in wrong conclusions
Technical difficulties integrating new systems
Cost of new hardware and software

Averaging data and measures of spread

Averaging measures

Mean
This is the average found by dividing the sum of values by the number of values.

Median
This is the middle value of a set of values.

Mode
This is the value which occurs most often.

Spread measures

Range
This is the highest data value minus the lowest data value of a set of data.

Standard deviation and variance
These are measures of how far the data points are from the mean.
variance = standard deviation^2

Coefficient of variation
This means a measure of the dispersion of the data points around the mean.
Calculated as:

$$\frac{\text{standard deviation}}{\text{mean}}$$

Averaging data example

Sample data: 1,120, 990, 1,040, 1,030, 1,105, 1,015

Mean $= \dfrac{\Sigma x}{n} = \dfrac{6,300}{6} = \underline{1,050}$ **Median** = middle observation

990, 1,015, 1,030, 1,040, 1,105, 1,120

median $= \dfrac{1,030 + 1,040}{2} = 1,035$

Frequency distribution

Output	f	x	fx
350-360	4	355	1,420
360-370	6	365	2,190
370-380	5	375	1,875
380-390	4	385	1,540
390-400	3	395	1,185
	22		8,210

x = midpoint of class

Mean $= \dfrac{\Sigma fx}{\Sigma f} = \dfrac{8,210}{22} = \underline{373}$

Measures of spread example

Range

What is the range of the values:

5, 7, 8, 8, 10?

Range = $10 - 5 = 5$

Coefficient of variation

Coefficient of variation $= \dfrac{\text{standard deviation}}{\text{mean}}$

$$= \dfrac{1.9}{5.045} = 38\%$$

mean $= \dfrac{\Sigma fx}{\Sigma f} = \dfrac{111}{22} = 5.045$

Standard deviation

Σ	f	fx	fx²
2	2	4	8
3	4	12	36
4	3	12	48
5	4	20	100
6	3	18	108
7	3	21	147
8	3	24	192
22	111	639	

$$sd = \sqrt{\dfrac{\Sigma fx^2}{\Sigma f} - \left(\dfrac{\Sigma fx}{\Sigma f}\right)^2}$$

$$= \sqrt{\dfrac{639}{22} - 5.045^2} = 1.9$$

Variance = standard deviation²

$$= 1.9^2 = 3.61$$

Risk and uncertainty

RISK describes a situation where we know the different possible outcomes and can estimate their associated probabilities.

UNCERTAINTY is used when we do not know the possible outcomes and/or their associated probabilities. Uncertainty is essentially a matter of ignorance.

Expected values and Probability

Probability is the likelihood of a given event occurring

If we can compile a complete list of all the equally likely outcomes, we can define the probability of an event, denoted P (event), as

$$P \text{ (event)} = \frac{\textbf{total number of outcomes which constitute the event}}{\textbf{total number of possible outcomes}}$$

Features of probability

- all lie between 0 (impossible) and 1 (certain)
- $P \text{ (not A)} = 1 - P \text{ (A)}$

Expected value is a long - run average

If an action has outcomes (x) with associated probabilities (p)

Expected value (EV) = Σpx

Example – daily sales figures

Sales (X)	probability	px
0	0.1	0
1	0.4	0.4
2	0.5	1.0
	1.0	1.4

The expected value is 1.4 sales

Normal distribution

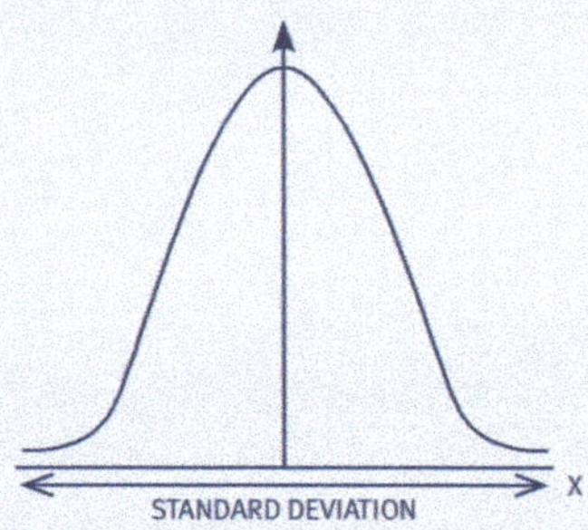

Features:

- Bell shaped
- Symmetrical
- Mean in the centre
- Total area under curve = 1

If we know the mean and the standard deviation, we can use the normal distribution to work out the percentage chance of a value occurring

Convert your variable to a **standard normal variable**

This has:
Mean (μ) = 0
Standard deviation (σ) = 1

$$Z = \frac{x - \mu}{\sigma}$$

Where:
Z = Z score
X = Value being considered

Standard normal curve

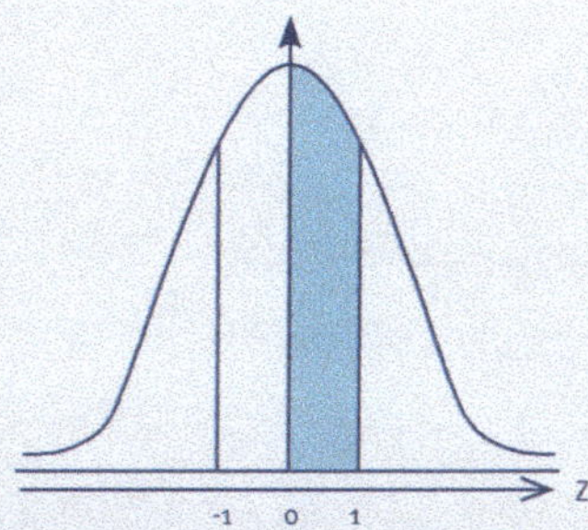

If Z score = 1
From the normal distribution
table = 0.3413 or 34.13%

So, 34.13% is the area from 0 to 1

It is also the area from –1 to 0

Example:

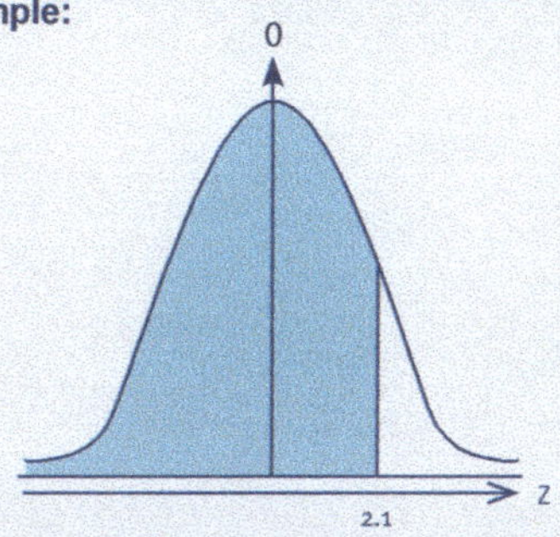

Find the probability that Z score is negative
or less than 2.1

$$P(Z \leftarrow 2.1) = 0.5 + TE\ (2.1)$$
$$= 0.5 + 0.4821$$
$$= 0.9821 = \underline{98.21\%}$$

(TE = table entry)

3

Presenting information

In this chapter

- Writing reports.
- Graphs and charts.

Exam focus

You will need to be able to interpret and do the relevant calculations for different types of graphs and charts.

Writing reports

Four stages:

1 Prepare

2 Plan

3 Write

4 Review

Structure:

- Title

- Introduction

- Analysis

- Conclusion

- Appendices

Graphs and charts

Simple bar chart

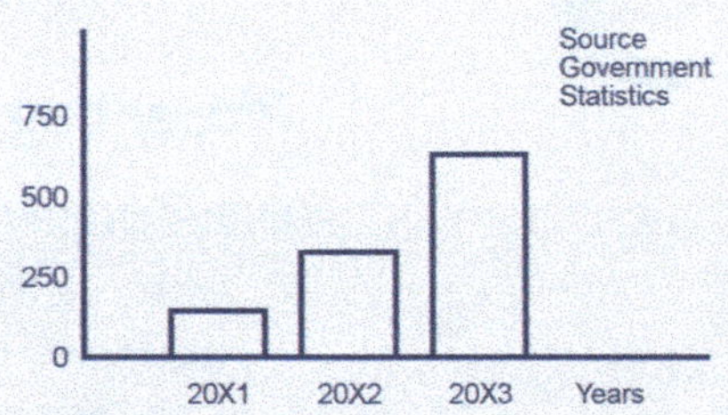

A simple bar chart is where one variable only is being illustrated.

Component bar chart

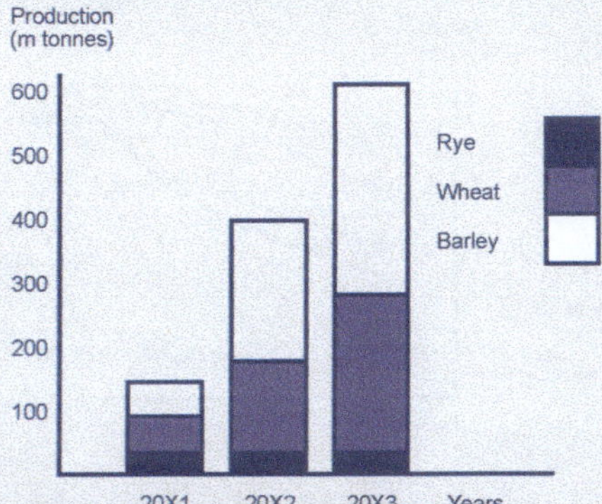

A component bar chart is used when each total figure in the data is made up of a number of different components and it is important that these component elements are shown as well as the total figure.

Percentage component bar chart

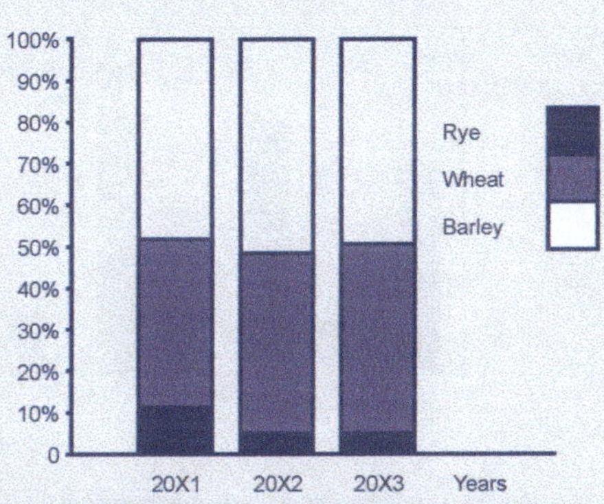

A percentage component bar chart is one where the actual values of each component are not shown but the percentage of the total for each component is. The bars in this type of chart are all the same height (representing 100%) and are split according to the proportions of each component element.

Compound bar chart

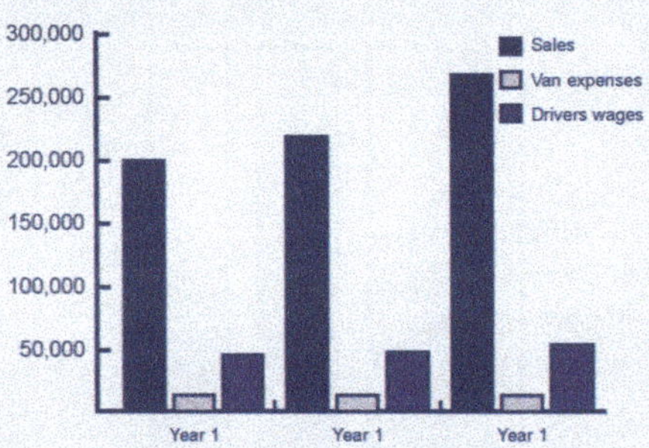

Multiple line chart

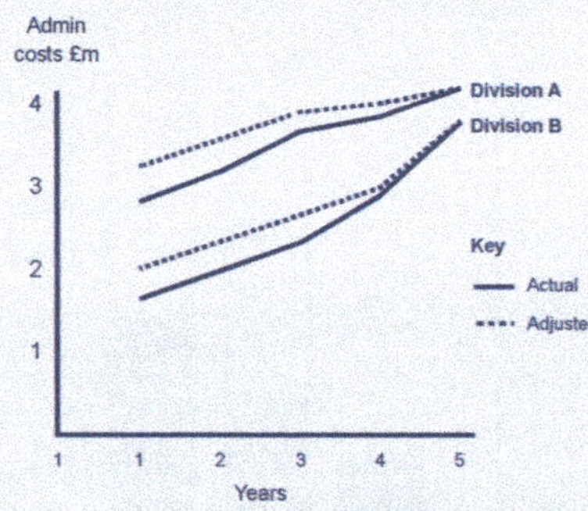

Compound bar charts are sometimes termed multiple bar charts. A compound bar chart is one where there is more than one bar for each subdivision of the chart.

It is a suitable format if the total of each component of the bar chart has no significance.

In many instances it will be found that data can be more clearly and understandably presented in the form of a line graph, especially if we are consider the change in an item over time.

Pie chart

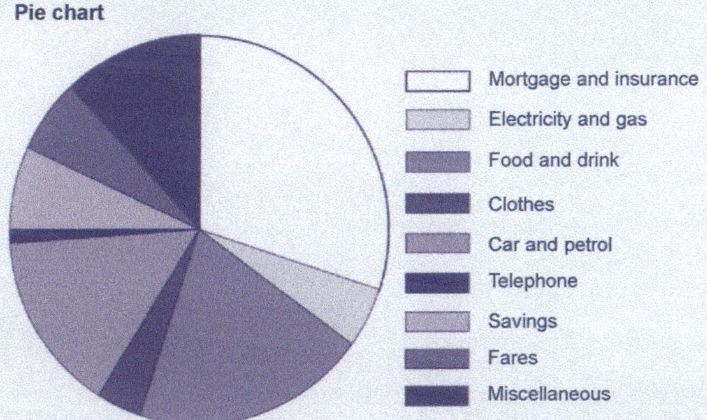

Constructing a pie chart

- Calculate the total value of all components of the numerical data
- Convert each component of data into 'degrees' of the circle:
  360°/Total value of the data = number of degrees per unit
- Calculate the size of the wedge required to represent each element of the data.

Cost classification

In this chapter

- Classifying costs.
- Element.
- Function.
- Nature.
- Behaviour.
- The high-low method – analysing costs into fixed and variable elements.
- Linear cost functions.
- Cost objects, units and centres.
- Cost coding.

It is vital that you understand the different ways of classifying and describing costs, and when a particular perspective is appropriate.

You also need to be aware of the high-low method as a way of splitting semi-variable costs into their fixed and variable components and the use of cost equations to estimate future costs.

Classifying costs

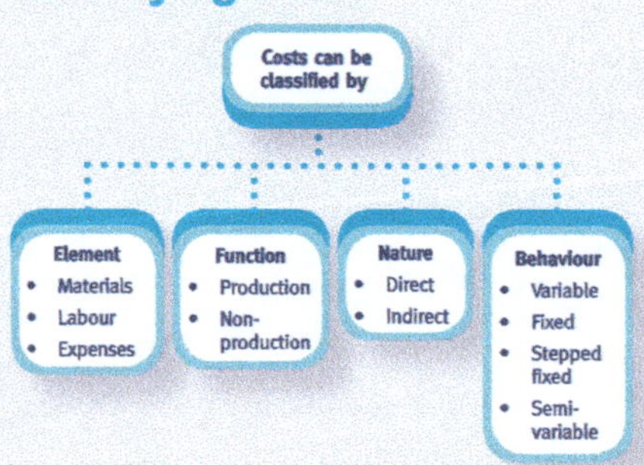

Element

Materials – all costs of materials purchased for production and non-production activities.

Labour – all staff costs relating to employees on the payroll of the organisation.

Expenses – all other costs which are not material or labour.

Function

Production costs are those incurred when raw materials are converted into finished and part-finished goods.

Non-production costs are costs not directly associated with the production processes in a manufacturing organisation.

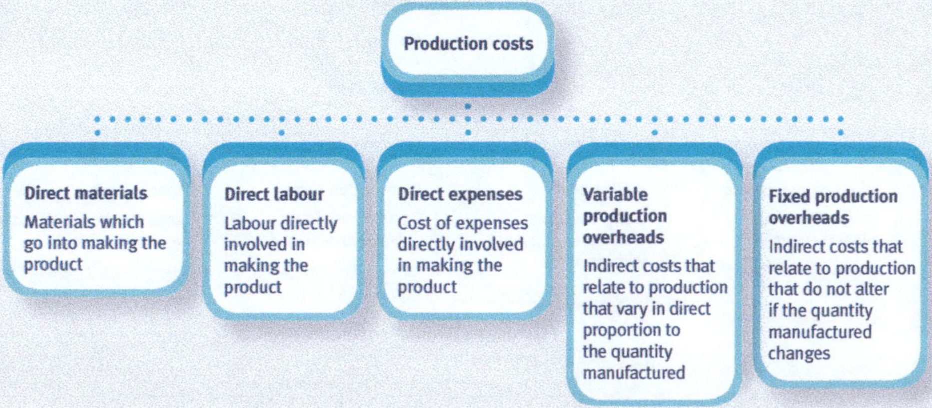

Production costs

Direct materials

Materials which go into making the product

Direct labour

Labour directly involved in making the product

Direct expenses

Cost of expenses directly involved in making the product

Variable production overheads

Indirect costs that relate to production that vary in direct proportion to the quantity manufactured

Fixed production overheads

Indirect costs that relate to production that do not alter if the quantity manufactured changes

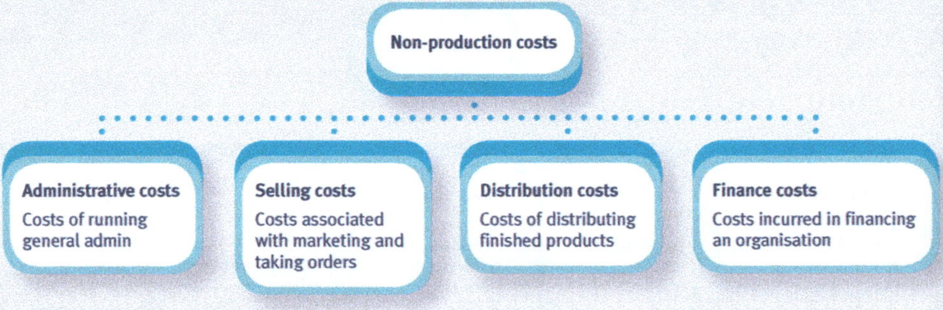

Non-production costs

Administrative costs

Costs of running general admin

Selling costs

Costs associated with marketing and taking orders

Distribution costs

Costs of distributing finished products

Finance costs

Costs incurred in financing an organisation

Nature

Definition

Direct costs

- Costs which can be directly identified with a specific unit or cost centre

- Total of direct costs = direct materials + direct labour + direct expenses = prime cost

Indirect costs

- Costs which cannot be directly identified to a specific unit or cost centre

- Indirect costs = indirect materials + indirect labour + indirect expenses = overheads

Behaviour

Cost behaviour is:

- the way in which input costs vary with different levels of activity

- understanding of cost behaviour central to budgeting, costing and decision making.

Variable cost

Definition

A cost that varies with the level of activity e.g. direct materials cost

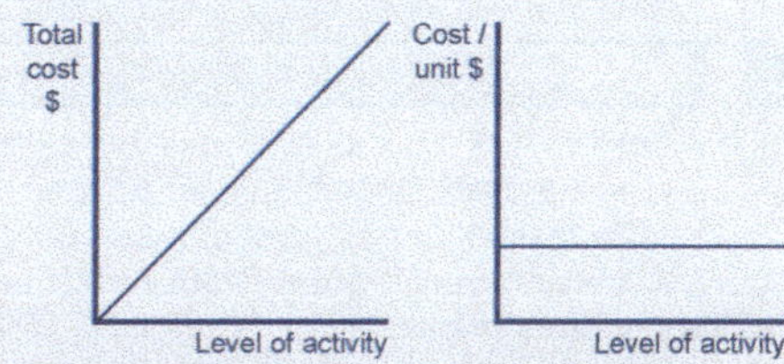

Fixed cost

Definition

A cost that is incurred for a period and that, within certain output and sales revenue limits, is unaffected by changes in the level of activity (output or sales revenue) e.g. factory rent.

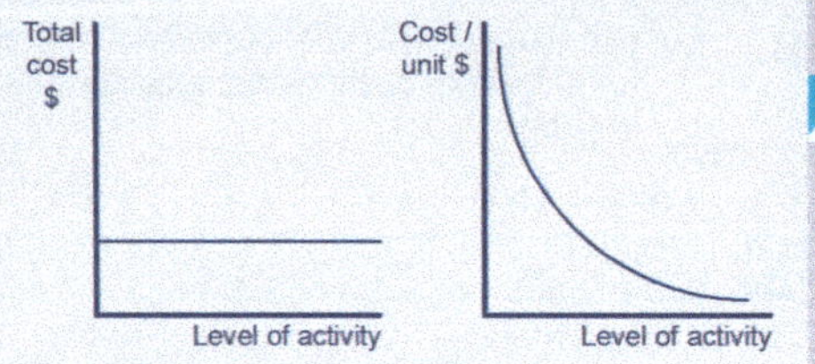

Stepped fixed cost

Definition

A fixed cost which is only fixed within certain levels of activity. Once the upper activity level is reached a new level of fixed cost becomes relevant e.g. warehouse costs and supervisors' wages.

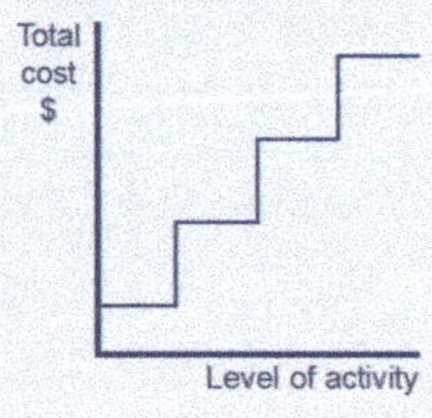

Semi-variable cost

Definition

Cost with a fixed and variable element e.g. telephone charges with fixed rental and charge per call.

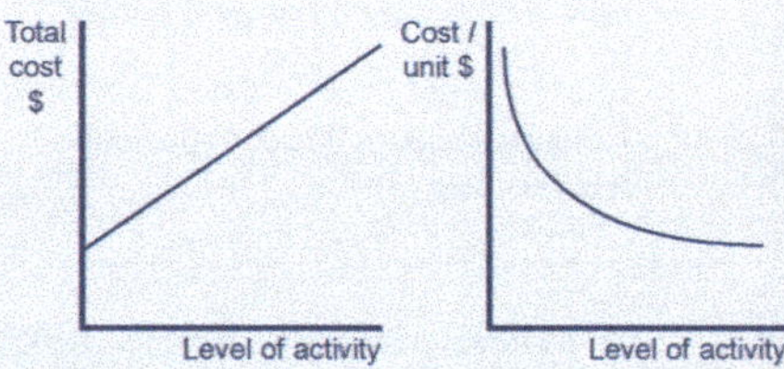

The high-low method – analysing costs into fixed and variable elements

Step 1: select high and low activity levels and their associated costs

Step 2: find variable cost per unit

Step 3: find fixed cost by substitution

$$\text{Variable cost per unit} = \frac{\text{Change in cost}}{\text{Change in level of activity}}$$

Fixed cost =   Total cost – total variable cost

- High-low method can still be used with care if there are stepped fixed costs or changes in the variable cost per unit.

Example

An organisation has following total costs at different activity levels.

Activity level (units)	4,000	6,000	8,000
Total cost ($)	105,000	150,000	190,000

There is a 20% step increase in fixed costs for each increase in activity level of 5,000 units.

Find the total cost of 4,500 units.

Solution

Calculate the variable cost per unit using two activity levels for which the fixed costs are the same. For example, both the 6,000 and 8,000 levels are within the 5,000 to 10,000 range:

Variable cost per unit =
(190,000 – 150,000) / (8,000 – 6,000) = $20

Total fixed cost above 5,000 units =
190,000 – 8,000 x 20 = $30,000

Total fixed cost below 5,000 units =
30,000 x 100/120 = 25,000

Total cost for 4,500 units =
25,000 + 4,500 x 20 = $115,000

Linear cost functions

Cost equations can be derived from historic data and then used to estimate future costs.

The total cost $y = a + bx$ where:

a = fixed cost per period
b = variable cost per unit
x = activity level

If fixed cost per period = $3,000 and variable cost per unit = $5

Then total cost per period $y = 3,000 + 5x$

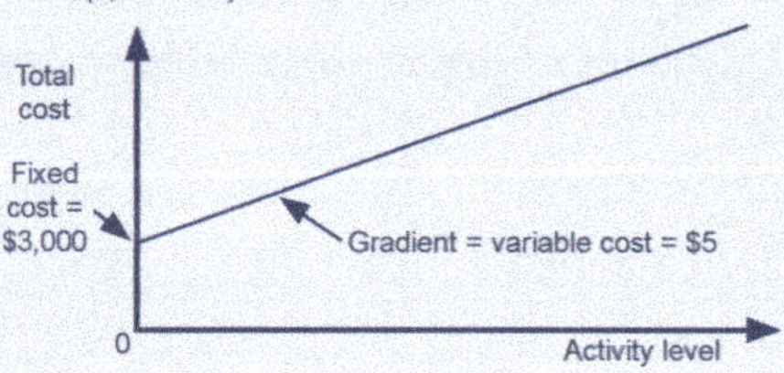

Example

The total cost of a product is given by the equation $y = 4,500 + 3.5x$.

The total fixed cost is $4,500

The variable cost is $3.50

The total cost for 100 units is
$(4,500 + 3.5 \times 100) = $4,850

Cost objects, units and centres

Definition

A **cost object** is any activity for which a separate measurement of cost is undertaken e.g. a product.

A **cost unit** is a unit of product or service in relation to which costs are ascertained e.g. a hotel room.

A **cost centre** is a production or service location, function, activity or item of equipment for which costs can be ascertained e.g. a ward in a hospital.

Cost cards

The **cost card** for a cost object, unit or centre brings together all the costs relating to it.

Example – cost card for a product

	$
Direct materials	X
Direct labour	X
Direct expenses	X
	—
PRIME COST	XX
Variable production overheads	X
	—
VARIABLE COST OF PRODUCTION	XX
Fixed production overheads	X
	—
TOTAL PRODUCTION COST	XX
Non-production overheads	X
	—
TOTAL COST OF A UNIT	XXX

Cost coding

A code is a system of symbols designed to be applied to a classified set of items, to give a brief accurate reference, which helps entry to the records, collation and analysis.

Coding systems

There are many ways to cost codes. Here are some of the more popular methods:

- Sequential Code – each code follows a numerical or alphabetical sequence

- Block Code – often used to categorise sequential codes together

- Hierarchical Code – each digit in the code represents a classification. As the code progresses from left to right each digit represents a smaller subset

- Significant digit code – is a code that contains individual digits and letters that are used to represent features of the coded item.

- Faceted Code – is a code that is broken down into a number of facets or fields, each of which signifies a unit of information.

5

Accounting for materials

In this chapter

- Ordering, receiving and issuing inventory.
- The costs of having inventory.
- Reorder levels.
- Economic order quantity.
- Economic batch quantity.
- Control procedures.
- Valuing inventory.
- The materials inventory account.

Exam focus

You need to understand the physical procedures for managing inventory as well as the method used for recording and accounting for it.

Ordering, receiving and issuing inventory

Ordering and purchasing

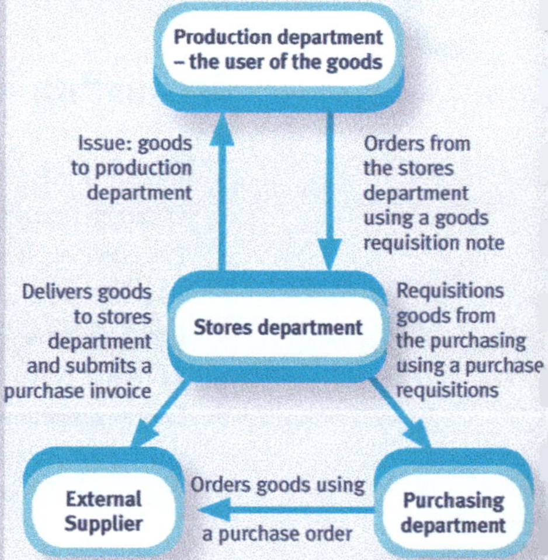

The paperwork

Document	Completed by	Sent to	Information included
Purchase requisition form	Production department	Purchasing department	Goods required Manager's authorisation
Purchase order form	Purchasing department	Supplier Accounting (copy) Goods receiving department (copy)	Goods required
Delivery note	Supplier	Goods receiving department	Check of goods delivered against order form
Goods received note	Goods receiving department	Purchasing department	Verification of goods received to enable payment
Materials requisition note	Production department	Stores	Authorisation to release goods Update stores records
Materials returned note	Production department	Stores	Details of goods returned to stores Update stores records
Materials transfer note	Production department A	Production department B	Goods transferred between departments Update stores records

You need to understand the costs associated with holding inventory and be able to calculate economic order quantities with and without discounts. The formulae will be given but make sure that you know how to use them.

The costs of having inventory

Holding costs – costs associated with holding inventory.

Holding costs	
Fixed holding costs	**Variable holding costs**
Cost of storage space	Interest on capital tied up in inventory
Cost of insurance	

Ordering costs – costs associated with placing orders.

- Administrative costs.

- Delivery costs.

- Order costs vary with number of orders placed.

Main objective of inventory control is to minimise total of holding, ordering and stock-out costs.

Reorder levels

Reorder level is the predetermined level of inventory at which order is placed.

To avoid the risk of stock-outs when demand during lead time to delivery is constant:

> Reorder level = usage x lead time

When lead time and demand in lead time is not constant:

> Reorder level = maximum usage x maximum lead time
>
> Maximum inventory level = reorder level + reorder quantity – (minimum usage x minimum lead time)
>
> Minimum inventory level (**buffer or safety stock**) = reorder level – (average usage x average lead time)
>
> Average inventory = (reorder quantity / 2) + minimum inventory

Economic order quantity

The economic order quantity minimises the total of ordering and holding costs.

$$\text{Economic order quantity} = Q = \sqrt{\frac{2C_O D}{C_H}}$$

Where:

D = demand per annum

C_O = cost of placing one order

C_H = cost of holding one unit per year

Annual ordering costs = $C_O \times D/Q$

Annual holding cost = $C_H \times Q/2$
(because it is assumed that average stock is half the order quantity)

Example

Annual demand = 125,000 units

Ordering cost = $10 per order

Holding cost = $0.10 per unit per annum

EOQ = $\sqrt{(2 \times 10 \times 125,000/0.10)}$ = 5,000 units

The EOQ with discounts for bulk ordering (bulk discounts)

Calculate the EOQ without discount

If EOQ is smaller than minimum for discount, calculate total annual costs of holding, ordering and purchase costs for EOQ

Calculate total costs for a reorder quantity just large enough to qualify for bulk discount

Compare total costs for both order quantities and select minimum cost alternative

Economic batch quantity

The economic batch quantity considers the number of manufactured items which should be produced in a batch to minimise the total costs.

- Cost of holding inventory.

- Cost of setting up batch ready for production.

$$EBQ = Q = \sqrt{\dfrac{2C_O D}{C_H\left(1-\dfrac{D}{R}\right)}}$$

Where:

D = demand per annum

C_O = cost of setting up batch

C_H = cost of holding one unit per year

R = annual replenishment (annual production) rate

Annual setup costs = $C_O \times D/Q$

Annual holding cost = $C_H \times Q/2(1-D/R)$

Control procedures

Perpetual inventory	Recording, as they occur, receipts, issues and the resulting balances of individual items of inventory in either quantity or quantity and value.
Periodic stocktaking	Checking balance of every item of inventory on the same date, usually at the end of an accounting period.
Continuous stocktaking	Counting and valuing selected items of inventory on a rotating basis. Specialist teams count and check certain inventory items on each day.
Slow-moving inventory	Those inventory items which take a long time to be used up.
Obsolete inventory	Those items of inventory which have become out of date and are no longer required.
Stores ledger card	Card used to update inventory records showing receipts, issues and orders.
Bin cards	Card showing a record of receipts, issues and balances of the quantity of an item of inventory handled by stores.

Other control procedures include:

- use of standard costs

- separation of ordering and purchasing

- checking all goods received

- delivery signatures

- physical security procedures.

Valuing inventory

FIFO (first in, first out)

Assumes that issues will be made from the oldest inventory available, leaving the latest purchases in inventory.

LIFO (last in, first out)

Assumes that issues will be made from the newest inventory available, leaving the earliest purchases in inventory.

Weighted average cost (AVCO)

Weighted average cost = Total cost of items in inventory/Number of items in inventory. Takes account of the relative quantities purchased at different prices in the cost per unit.

The materials inventory account

Materials inventory account	
Debit entries – increase in inventory	**Credit entries – decrease in inventory**
Opening inventory (opening balance)	Work-in-progress (direct materials used)
Payables (materials purchased on credit)	Materials returned to suppliers
	Production overheads (indirect materials used)
Materials returned to stores	Statement of profit or loss (material write-offs)
	Closing inventory (closing balance)

Item	Debit entry	Credit entry
Materials purchased on credit	Materials inventory account	Payables
Materials returned to stores	Materials inventory account	Work-in-progress account
Direct materials used in production	Work-in-progress account	Materials inventory account
Materials returned to suppliers	Payables	Materials inventory account
Indirect materials used	Production overheads	Materials inventory account
Materials written-off	Statement of profit or loss	Materials inventory account

6

Accounting for labour

In this chapter

- Direct and indirect labour costs.
- Accounting for labour costs.
- Remuneration methods.
- Labour turnover.
- Labour related ratios.

Exam focus

There are two key areas when considering labour costs:

- determining the wages bill to be paid

- splitting the labour cost between its direct and indirect elements.

Specific details of remuneration schemes will be given in the question. Read it carefully and do exactly what it says.

Direct and indirect labour costs

Type of worker	Direct labour cost	Indirect labour cost
Workers directly involved in making products	Basic pay Overtime premium on specific job at customer's request	General overtime premium Bonus payments Idle time Sick pay Time spent on indirect jobs
Indirect workers • Maintenance staff • Supervisors • Canteen staff		All costs

Accounting for labour costs

Labour account	
Debit entry	**Credit entries**
Bank – labour costs incurred	Work-in-progress – direct labour costs
	Production overheads – indirect labour costs

Remuneration methods

The specific details of schemes will be given in the question. Read it carefully.

Time based schemes

Total wages = (hours worked x basic rate of pay per hour) + (overtime hours worked x overtime premium per hour).

Time based schemes:

- can result in higher quality as workers are happy to spend longer on units to get them right

- some workers may take longer just to get paid more. There is no incentive to improve productivity.

Piecework schemes

Total wages = number of units completed x agreed rate per unit.

Piecework schemes:

- may involve a guaranteed minimum wage

- may use higher rate per unit once productivity target is achieved

- may result in higher productivity at the expense of quality.

Other schemes

Many involve flat salary plus bonus.

Bonus schemes

- Can be aimed at individuals and/ or groups.

- Use many different systems.

Example

A company operates a premium bonus scheme for its employees of 50% of the time saved compared with the standard time allowance for a job, at the normal hourly rate. The data relating to Job 999 completed by an employee is as follows:

Allowed time for Job 999 12 hours

Time taken to complete Job 999 10 hours

Normal hourly rate of pay $15

What is the total pay of the employee for the 10 hours spent on Job 999?

Solution

Time saved = 12 – 10 = 2 hours

Bonus paid = $0.50 x 2 hours x $15 = $15

Basic pay for time worked=10 hours x $15=$150

Total pay =$165

Labour turnover

Definition

Labour turnover is a measure of the proportion of people leaving compared to those employed.

Labour turnover for a given period =

$$\frac{\text{Number of leavers who require replacement}}{\text{Average number of employees}} \times 100\%$$

Labour related ratios

Definition

Labour efficiency ratio measures performance by comparing actual time taken to do the job with the expected time.

Labour efficiency ratio =

$$\frac{\text{Standard hours worked to produce actual output}}{\text{Actual hours worked to produce actual output}} \times 100\%$$

Definition

Labour capacity ratio compares numbers of hours spent actively working with total hours available.

Labour capacity ratio =

$$\frac{\text{Actual hours worked to produce actual output}}{\text{Total budgeted hours}} \times 100\%$$

Definition

Labour production volume ratio compares numbers of hours expected to be worked to produce actual output with total hours available for work.

Labour production volume ratio =

$$\frac{\text{Standard hours to produce actual output}}{\text{Total budgeted hours}} \times 100\%$$

Definition

Standard hour = A standard hour can be used to state the number of production units which should be achieved within a period of one hour.

Example

Actual output in period	250 units
Actual hours worked	420 hours
Standard time allowed per unit	90 minutes
Budgeted hours	450 hours

Solution

Standard hours to make actual output = 250 units x 90/60 = 375 hours

Labour efficiency ratio = 375/420 x 100 = 89%

Labour capacity ratio = 420/450 x 100 = 93%

Labour production volume ratio = 375/450 x 100 = 83%

7

Accounting for overheads

In this chapter

- Overheads and absorption costing.
- Cost allocation and apportionment.
- Reapportionment.
- Absorption.
- Under- and over-absorption.
- Ledger accounting for overheads.

Exam focus

If a question asks you to calculate the total cost of a product, deal with the direct costs and then the overheads.

When a question asks about overheads, check how much of the following diagram needs to be worked through.

You may also need to understand how to choose a suitable base for apportionment.

Step 1:

Overheads allocated or apportioned to cost centres using suitable bases

Step 2:

Service centre costs reapportioned to production centres

Step 3:

Overheads absorbed into units of production

Units of production

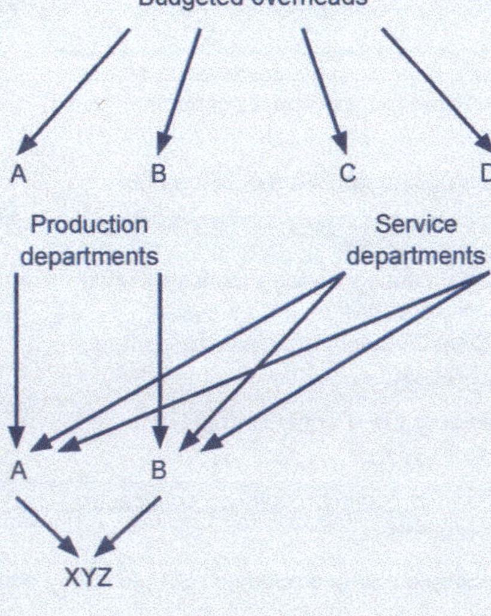

Overheads and absorption costing

> **Definition**
>
> Overheads are indirect costs which cannot be identified to a particular cost unit or cost centre.
>
> • Overheads may be fixed or variable.

> **Definition**
>
> Absorption costing is the process by which production overheads are recovered by absorbing them into a product by a three stage process:
>
> • allocation and apportionment of overheads
>
> • reapportionment of service cost centre overheads
>
> • absorption of overheads.

Cost allocation and apportionment

> **Definition**
>
> **Allocation** is the charging of overheads directly to specific departments where they can be identified directly with a cost centre or cost unit.

> **Definition**
>
> **Apportionment** is the sharing of overheads which relate to more than one department between those departments on a fair basis.
>
> • The apportionment should be in proportion to the benefit received.

Reapportionment

Service department costs need to be reapportioned to the production departments.

- This should be done using a suitable basis linked to usage of the service.

- Step down apportionment is used when one service department works or provides a service for other service departments as well as the production departments. The service department that provides services for more departments is reapportioned first.

- The main complication here is having multiple service departments with reciprocal usage. The easiest way to deal with this is to repeatedly reapportion overheads out of service departments until the figures are no longer material.

Example of reciprocal apportionment

The total overheads allocated and apportioned to the production and service departments of LS Ltd are as follows.

Assembly = $17,350

Finishing = $23,970

Maintenance = $18,600

Canteen = $6,600

A suitable basis for sharing out the maintenance costs is the time spent servicing equipment. The amount of time spent by the maintenance department servicing equipment in the other three departments has been analysed as follows.

Assembly	50%
Finishing	40%
Canteen	10%

The Canteen department's overheads are to be reapportioned on the basis of the number of employees in the other three departments.

	Assembly	Finishing	Maintenance	Canteen
Number of employees	18	30	12	2

Solution

	Assembly $	Finishing $	Maintenance $	Canteen $	Total $
Total from above	17,350	23,970	18,600	6,600	66,520
Reapportion canteen	1,980	3,300	1,320	(6,600)	–
Reapportion maintenance	9,960	7,968	(19,920)	1,992	–
Reapportion canteen	598	996	398	(1,992)	–
Reapportion maintenance	199	159	(398)	40	–
Reapportion canteen	12	20	8	(40)	–
Reapportion maintenance	4	3	(8)	1	–
Reapportion canteen	0	1	–	(1)	–
Total	30,103	36,417	0	0	66,520

Absorption

> **Definition**

Absorption is the process whereby costs within cost centres are charged to a cost unit.

Different bases can be used:

- labour or machine hours (the most common approach)
- percentage of direct labour cost
- percentage of material cost
- percentage of prime cost
- cost per unit (gives a blanket overhead cost per unit for all products).

Overhead absorption rate = OAR = budgeted overheads / budgeted level of activity.

Under and over-absorption

If overheads are absorbed throughout a period using the predetermined overhead absorption rate, at the end of the period there may be a difference between the overheads absorbed and the actual overhead incurred.

Using direct labour hours:

Overhead absorbed = actual direct labour hours x OAR	X
Actual overhead incurred	X
Difference = overhead under- or over-absorbed	?

There are two main reasons for this difference:

- actual overheads different from budget
- actual activity level different from budget.

If overheads have been under-absorbed, then they have not all been accounted for and an additional debit is needed in the statement of profit or loss to account for the difference.

If overheads have been over-absorbed, then too high a value of overheads has been accounted for and an additional credit is needed in the statement of profit or loss to cancel out that effect.

> **Exam focus**

Sometimes you may be given information relating to the actual **under-absorption** or **over-absorption** in a period and be expected to calculate the budgeted overheads or the actual number of hours worked. As long as you remember the basic formula involved in calculating under- or over-absorption, you shouldn't have any problems.

Ledger accounting for overheads

Production Overheads

	£		£
Actual Overhead cost (1)		Absorbed overheads (2)	
Over-absorbed (3)		Under-absorbed (4)	

(1) The **actual cost** of all the indirect costs is recorded as a **debit** in the production overheads account. The credit is either in the bank or payables account. The actual cost will be made up of all the indirect production costs – material, labour and expenses.

(2) The overheads that are **absorbed into production** (WIP) are recorded as a **credit** in the production overheads account. This is calculated as the **budgeted OAR x actual activity**

(3) When the account is balanced at the end of the period and the **balancing amount** is required to make the **debit** side of the account match the credit side we have an **over-absorption** of overheads.

(4) When the account is balanced at the end of the period and the **balancing amount** is required to make the **credit** side of the account match the debit side we have an **under-absorption** of overheads.

8

Absorption and marginal costing

In this chapter

- The concept of contribution.
- Absorption and marginal costing.
- Arguments for the different approaches.

Exam focus

The concept of contribution is very important as this is at the heart of marginal costing and the decision-making process. You also need to be able to reconcile the different profit figures using marginal and absorption costing.

The concept of contribution

Definition

The marginal cost of a unit of product is the total of the variable costs of the product.

- It is the additional cost of producing an extra unit of the product.

Definition

Contribution = sales price – variable cost
Profit = contribution – fixed cost

Contribution per unit of product:

- gives an idea of how much money there is available to contribute towards paying for the overheads of the organisation.

- is usually assumed to be constant at varying levels of output and sales.

chapter 8

Absorption and marginal costing

	Absorption costing	Marginal costing
Valuing units	Units are valued at total production cost	Units are valued at marginal (variable production) cost
Valuing inventory	Opening and closing inventory are valued at total production cost	Opening and closing inventory are valued at marginal cost
Treatment of fixed production overheads	Carried forward from one period to another as part of the closing (opening) inventory valuation. They only hit the profit figure when units are sold	Fixed costs are charged in full against profit in the period in which they are incurred
Adjusting for under- or over-absorption	An adjustment for under- or over-absorption of overheads is made in the statement of profit or loss	No adjustment for under- or over-absorption of overheads needed

	Absorption costing	**Marginal costing**
Impact of increase in inventory level	Gives higher profit	Gives lower profit
Impact of decrease in inventory level	Gives lower profit	Gives higher profit
Inventory level constant	Same profit with both systems	

Note: the difference in profit is due solely to the different opening and closing inventory values, which is due to the treatment of fixed production overheads. It has nothing to do with under- or over-absorption of overheads.

Reconciliation statement

Absorption costing profit	X
Change in inventory x FOAR	+/-X
Marginal costing profit	X

Marginal costing profit statement

Sales revenue = units sold x price	X
Less cost of sales = units sold x marginal cost of a unit	(X)
Less variable non-production costs actually incurred	(X)
Contribution	XX
Less fixed production costs actually incurred	(X)
Less fixed non-production costs actually incurred	(X)
Net profit/(loss)	XX

Absorption costing profit statement

Sales revenue = units sold x price	X
Less cost of sales = units sold x full production cost of a unit	(X)
Over/ (under) absorption	X
Gross profit	XX
Less variable non-production costs actually incurred	(X)
Less fixed non-production costs actually incurred	(X)
Net profit/(loss)	XX

Arguments for the different approaches

Advantages of marginal costing	Advantages of absorption costing
• Contribution per unit is constant unlike profit per unit which varies with changes in sales volumes. • There is no under or over absorption of overheads (and hence no adjustment is required in the statement of profit or loss). • Fixed costs are a period cost and are charged in full to the period under consideration. • Marginal costing is useful in the decision making process. • It is simple to operate.	• Absorption costing includes an element of fixed overheads in inventory values (in accordance with accounting standards). • Analysing under/over absorption of overheads is a useful exercise in controlling costs of an organisation. • In small organisations, absorbing overheads into the costs of products is the best way of estimating job costs and profits on jobs.

9

Job, batch and process costing

In this chapter

- Job costing.
- Batch costing.
- Overview of process costing.
- Process costing with gains and losses.
- Work-in-progress (equivalent units).
- Losses made part way through production.
- Joint and by-products.

Exam focus

The key to service, job and batch costing is to treat them like any other normal costing exercise – deal with direct costs first and then look at how to apportion/absorb overheads.

Well laid out workings and a systematic approach are critical to process costing questions.

Job costing

The key feature of job costing is that each job is unique.

- Produce a cost card for each individual job to find out the costs that will be incurred.

- All the same principles of costing should be used.

The total cost of the job is made up as:

	$
Direct materials	X
Direct labour	X
Direct expenses	X
Overheads absorbed	X
TOTAL COST	XX

Profit may be a mark-up on cost or a margin (percentage of price).

- Check carefully to make sure you are using the correct formula.

Batch costing

The key feature of batch costing is that each batch is different, but within each batch all items are identical.

The costing process has two steps.

1   Determine the total cost of the batch, effectively treating each batch as a job in its own right.

2   Cost per unit = total batch costs / number of units in the batch.

Some costs, such as design or set-up costs, may be fixed regardless of the size of the batch; others will vary with the number of units in the batch.

Overview of process costing

Process costing is used where production is continuous, making it difficult to identify conventional, separate units of production. Common features of process costing are as follows.

- A series of separate processes is required to manufacture the finished product. The output of one process becomes the input of the next process.

- Where there is closing work-in-progress (WIP) at the end of one period this forms the opening WIP at the beginning of the next period.

- There are often losses in the process, so output from a process does not equal input.

- There may be part-finished units at the end of the period.

- There may be by-products and joint products.

Our objectives are to find a cost per unit of output and to value closing inventories.

Process costing with gains and losses

Normal losses

A **normal loss** is one that is expected to occur.

- Normal losses do not pick up a share of the process costs – all process costs go into the expected output.

- Losses may sometimes be sold for scrap value. The proceeds can be credited against the cost of the output.

Example

Input 1,000 units.

Production costs $5,800

Scrap units equal to 5% of input are expected, giving a normal loss of 50 units. Scrap can be sold for $2 per unit.

Average cost per unit (always calculated using expected figures)

= (total costs of inputs – scrap value of normal loss) / (units input – normal loss)

= (5,800 – 50 x 2) / (1,000 – 50)

= $6

Abnormal loss

An **abnormal loss** occurs when actual losses are greater than expected losses.

- Abnormal losses pick up a share of the cost and are valued at the same cost per unit as good output.

- Abnormal losses are written off in the statement of profit or loss, via an abnormal loss amount.

- Cost of the abnormal loss is reduced by scrap value of the abnormally lost units.

Example

In the previous example, suppose output was only 940 units rather than the 950 expected.

There would therefore be 10 units of abnormal loss.

The good output and the abnormal loss would be costed at $6 per unit. That figure is not changed because of abnormal losses. The $6 is arrived at assuming everything goes as expected.

In the statement of profit or loss, however, the cost of the abnormal loss would be reduced by the extra scrap proceeds giving a charge of 10 x (6-2) = $40.

Abnormal gain

An abnormal gain occurs when the actual loss in period is less than expected.

- Abnormal gains are treated like abnormal losses but debits and credits are reversed.

- Benefit credited to statement of profit or loss, less any reduction from being unable to sell the scrap that isn't there because of the abnormal gain.

Steps for answering questions:

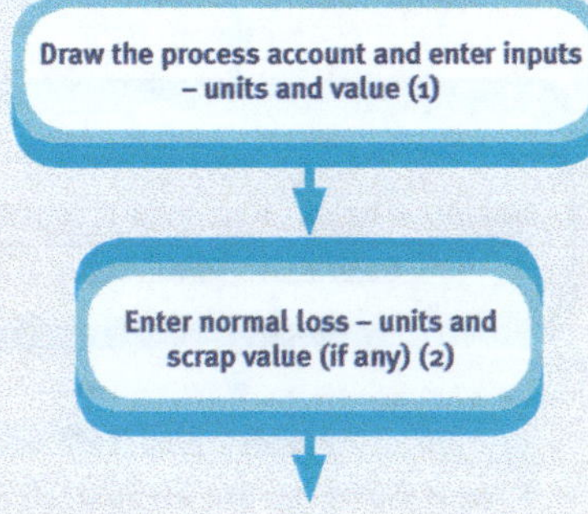

Enter good output – units only (3)

↓

Balance units – balancing figure is abnormal loss or gain. (4)

↓

Calculate the average cost per unit:

$$\frac{\text{Total cost of inputs} - \text{scrap value of normal loss}}{\text{Units input} - \text{normal loss}}$$

↓

Value good output and abnormal loss or gain at average cost per unit. (5)

↓

Transfer the normal loss to the scrap account and the abnormal loss to the abnormal loss/gain account and then onto the scrap account (6)

↓

Balance the normal loss account to the cash figure received. Balance the abnormal loss/gain account for the true loss/benefit received. (7)

Example

Using the figures from example above:

Process account

	units	$		units	$
Inputs (1)	1,000	5,800	Normal loss (2,6) ($2)	50	100
			Abnormal loss (4,5,6) ($6)	10	60
			Finished output (3,5) ($6)	940	5,640
	1,000	5,800		1,000	5,800

Scrap account

Normal loss (6)	100	Cash (7)		120
Abnormal loss (6)	20			

Abnormal loss/gain account

Abnormal loss from process account (10 units @ $6 each) (6)	60	Abnormal loss transferred to scrap account (10 units @ $2 each) (6)	20
		Abnormal loss transferred to the Statement of profit or loss (7)	40

Work-in-progress (equivalent units)

When there are incomplete units at the beginning or end of the period the concept of equivalent units (EUs) is used.

- A part-processed unit is expressed as a proportion of a fully-completed unit e.g 100 half-completed units are effectively equal to 50 fully-completed units.

- The use of EUs means process costs can be spread fairly between fully completed and part-processed units.

- For most processes, material is input at the start of the process, so material cost is spread over all units but conversion costs are spread over the EUs.

- Work-in-progress can be valued using weighted average costing of production or first-in-first-out.

Example

Opening WIP

- 10 units, 70% complete for materials and 80% for conversion

- cost $323 ($148 materials, $175 conversion)

Units transferred in from previous process during this period;

- 90 units

- Cost of $200 (all materials)

Closing WIP:

- 20 units

- 60% complete for materials and 75% for conversion

Additional period costs:

- materials $480

- conversion costs $870

Method 1 – weighted average cost of production (AVCO)

Under AVCO, opening inventory values added to current costs to provide overall average cost per unit.

Process account

	units	$		units	$
Opening WIP	10	323	Completed units (balance)	80	100
Transfer from previous process	90	200			
			Closing WIP	20	273
Materials	–	480			
Conversion	–	870			
	100	1,873		100	1,873

<table>
<tr><td colspan="6">Working 1: number of equivalent units produced</td></tr>
<tr><td></td><td>Units</td><td colspan="2">Materials</td><td colspan="2">Conversion</td></tr>
<tr><td></td><td></td><td>% complete</td><td>Equivalent units</td><td>% complete</td><td>Equivalent units</td></tr>
<tr><td>Completed units</td><td>80</td><td>100</td><td>80</td><td>100</td><td>80</td></tr>
<tr><td>Closing WIP</td><td>20</td><td>60</td><td>12</td><td>75</td><td>15</td></tr>
<tr><td>TOTAL UNITS</td><td></td><td></td><td>92</td><td></td><td>95</td></tr>
</table>

Working 2: Cost per equivalent unit

Materials cost per equivalent unit = all materials costs / equivalent units

= (148 + 200 + 480) / 92 = $9

Conversion cost per equivalent unit = all conversion costs / equivalent units

= (175 + 870) / 95 = $11

Working 3: Apply costs to equivalent units

	Materials (Materials EU x materials cost per EU)	Conversion (conversion EU x conversion cost per EU)	Valuation $
Completed units	80 x 9	80 x 11	1,600
Closing WIP	12 x 9	15 x 11	273
Total			1,873

Note that the total value of closing inventory $1,873 agrees with the total costs input in the process account.

Method 2 – FIFO

Under FIFO we assume that opening WIP units are competed first. Process costs in period allocated between:

- opening WIP units

- units started and completed in the period (fully-worked units)

- closing WIP units

Therefore, of the 80 units finished, a distinction is made between those which were started and finished in the period (70 units), and those which were started last period and finished this period (10 units).

Process account

	units	$		units	$
Opening WIP	10	323	Opening WIP (now finished)	10	367
Transfer from previous process	90	200	Units started and finished in the period	70	1,260
Materials	-	480	Closing WIP	20	246
Conversion	-	870			
	100	1,873		100	1,873

Working 1: number of equivalent units

	Units	Materials		Conversion	
		% complete	Equivalent units	% complete	Equivalent units
Opening WIP (finished this period)	10	30	3*	20	2*
Units started and finished in the period	70	100	70	100	70
Closing WIP	20	60	12	75	15
TOTAL UNITS			85		87

* Opening WIP comprises 10 units 70% complete with respect to material. Therefore, this period, finishing off those items is equivalent to 10 x (100% - 70%) = 3 whole units.

Opening WIP comprises 10 units 80% complete with respect to conversion. Therefore, this period, finishing off those items is equivalent to 10 x (100% - 80%) = 2 whole units.

Working 2: Cost per equivalent unit:

Materials cost per equivalent unit = all materials costs for the period /equivalent units for the period = (200 + 480) / 85 = $8

Conversion cost per equivalent unit = all conversion costs for the period / equivalent units for the period = 870 / 87 = $10

Working 3: Apply costs to equivalent units

	Materials (Materials EU x materials cost per EU)	Conversion (conversion EU x conversion cost per EU)	Valuation $
Opening WIP (finishing)	3 x 8	2 x 10	44
Starting and finishing	70 x 8	70 x 10	1,260
Closing WIP	12 x 8	15 x 10	246

Note:total cost of opening WIP (finished) = costs b/f + period costs = 323 + 44 = 367

Losses made part way through production

It is possible for losses to be identified part way through a process. In this case EUs must be used to assess the extent to which costs were incurred at the time when the loss was identified.

> **Calculate the normal loss and abnormal loss or gain.**

> **Calculate the expected number of EUs**
> **Expected output is actual finished units + abnormal loss**

> **Calculate the cost per EU**
> **Used to value finished units plus abnormal loss**

> **Write up process accounts and normal and abnormal loss accounts**

Example

The following information is available for a production process for the last period:

Material input	100 kg at $5 per kg
Labour and overhead input	$1,500
Transfer to finished goods	75 kg

Normal loss is 20% of input. Losses are identified when the process is 40% complete.

There is no opening or closing work-in-progress and lost units have no scrap value.

Prepare the process and normal and abnormal loss accounts for the period.

1 Normal loss is 20% of input = 20kg.
   Actual loss = 25 kg
   Abnormal loss = 5 kg.

2 Equivalent units of output:

	Units	EUs – Materials	EUs – Conversion
Finished output	75	100% 75	100% 75
Abnormal loss	5	100% 5	40% 2
Total EUs		80	77
Costs		$500	$1, 500
Costs per EU		$500/80kg = $6.25	$1,500/77kg = $19.48
Total cost of completed unit		$6.25 + $19.48 = $25.73	

Value of finished output = 75 units @$25.73 per unit = $1,930

Total cost of abnormal loss per unit = ($6.25 x 5 units) + ($19.48 x 2 units) = $70.21

4 Process account

Process account

	units	$		units	$
Materials	100	500	Normal loss	20	–
Labour and overheads		1,500	Finished goods	75	1,930
			Abnormal loss	5	70
	100	2,000		100	2,000

Normal loss account

	units	$		units	$
Process account	20	–	Scrap – Nil value	20	–

Abnormal loss account

	units	$		units	$
Process account	5	70	Statement of profit or loss	5	70
	5	70		5	70

Joint and by-products

Definition

Joint products are:

- two or more products, indistinguishable until the split-off point, each having a sufficiently high saleable value to be recognised as a main product

- costs before the split-off point are common to all products and are called **joint costs** or **common costs**.

Definition

By-products are:

- output of insignificant value produced with joint products.

Accounting treatment

Joint products	By-products

• Joint costs apportioned between the joint products at split-off point to obtain the cost of each product to value inventory and cost of sales
 	
• Basis of apportionment usually one of:
 	
   – sales value of production
 	
   – production units
 	
   – net realisable value
	Non-cost methods
	
	• Other income – The net sales of by-products for the current period is recognised as Other Income.
	
	• By-product revenue deducted from the main product(s) cost – The net sales of value of the by-products will be treated as a deduction from the cost of the main product.
	
	Cost Methods of Accounting for By-Products
	
	• Replacement Cost Method values the by-product inventory at its opportunity cost of purchasing or replacing the by-products.
	
	• Total Costs Less By-Products Valued at Standard Price Method – By-products are valued at a standard price to avoid fluctuations in by-product value.
	
	• Joint Cost Pro-rata Method allocates some of the joint cost to the by-product using any one of the joint cost allocation methods. This method is rarely used in practice.

Example

A company produces two joint products, A and B, and one by-product C. There are no costs specifically identifiable to product B:

	$ A	$ B	$ Total
Revenue	X	X	X
Costs identifiable to individual products	(X)	–	(X)
Net realisable value	XX	XX	XX
Common costs less profit from the by-product	(X)	(X)	(X)
Profit	XX	XX	XX

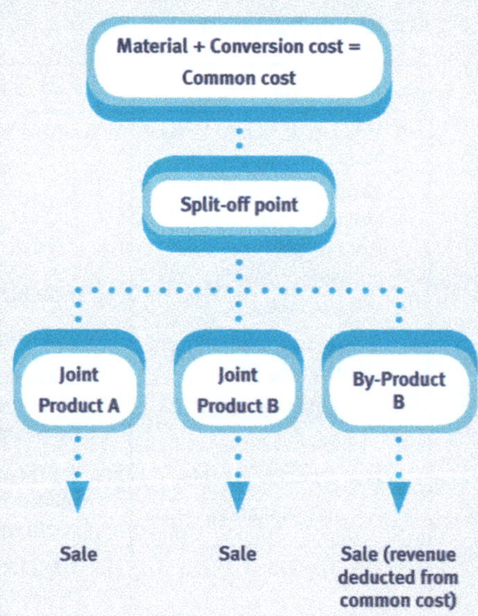

Service and operation costing

In this chapter

- The nature of service and operation costing.
- Suitable cost units.
- Service cost analysis.

Determining costs for services is just like any other costing exercise but with the added complication of the selection of a suitable cost unit.

The nature of service and operation costing

Four main differences between the output of **service industries** and products of manufacturing industries:

- intangibility – output cannot be touched or examined

- heterogeneity – nature of output is variable due to high human input and the nature of many services

- simultaneous production and consumption – service cannot be inspected before receiving it

- perishability – services cannot be stored.

Suitable cost units

There are no set rules for selecting service cost units.

- cost units should be based on their relevance to the service provided

- may be necessary to use composite cost units

- it is often useful in service organisations to calculate more than one different type of cost unit to enable cost control.

Example

Service	Possible cost unit
Hotel	Cost per guest per night
Transport	Cost per passenger mile
College	Cost per student
Hospital	Cost per patient day
	Cost per procedure

Service cost analysis

All the same principles of costing should be used. This means that the total cost per unit (whatever the unit happens to be) is still made up as:

	$
Direct materials	X
Direct labour	X
Direct expenses	X
Overheads absorbed	X
TOTAL COST	XX

$$\text{Cost per service unit} = \frac{\text{Total costs for providing service}}{\text{Number of service units used to provide the service}}$$

The key characteristics of service product costs are:

- labour may be the only direct cost

- overheads usually make up the bulk of the cost and are likely to be absorbed using direct labour hours.

Alternative costing principles

In this chapter

- Activity based costing.
- Target costing.
- Life cycle costing.
- Product life cycle.
- Total quality management (TQM).

This chapter covers some alternative forms of costing. It is important to understand the concepts for each of these.

Activity based costing

ABC is a form of absorption costing but rather than absorbing overheads on a production volume basis (such as hours worked) it allocates costs into cost pools and then absorbs them using cost drivers.

Cost pool – an activity that consumes resources and for which overhead costs are identified and allocated.

Cost driver – a unit of activity that consumes resources or the factor that influences the level of cost.

Advantages	Disadvantages
• More accurate cost per unit • Better pricing strategy • More information on what causes a cost • Can be applied to all overheads not just production overheads	• Only of benefit is overheads are significant • Some arbitrary allocation will still have to made • Complex procedure therefore time consuming and costly

Target costing

Is a cost estimate derived by subtracting a desired profit from a competitive market price. Often cost will need to be reduced to be able to achieve the target.

Value analysis is a systematic examination of factors affecting the cost of a product or service, in order to devise means of achieving the specified purpose most economically.

Value engineering attempts to design the best possible value at the lowest possible cost into a new product.

Life cycle costing

This technique compares the revenues from a product with all the costs incurred over the entire product life cycle. This enables:

- Profitability to be forecast for a product over its entire life.

- Costs to be compared at any stage of the products life cycle.

Product life cycle

Sales/profit

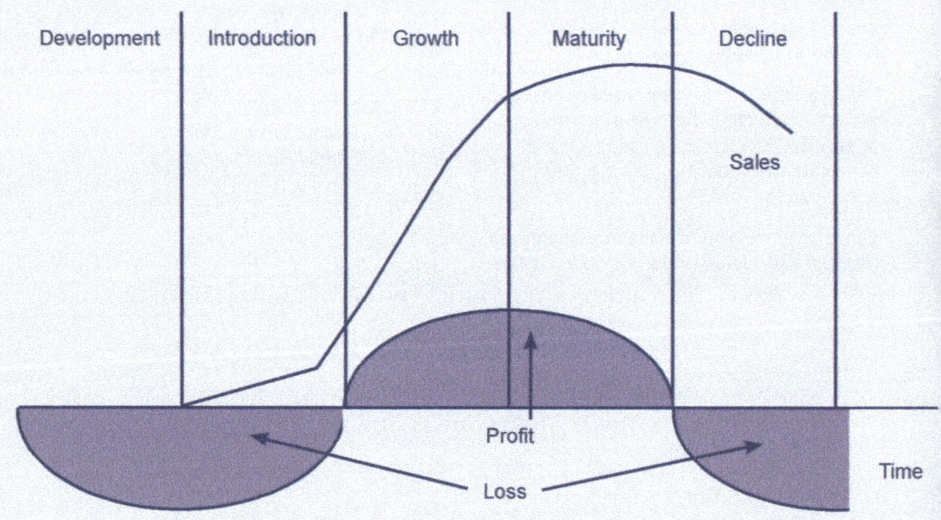

Total Quality Management (TQM)

- Total – means that everyone in the value chain is involved in the process, including employees, customer and suppliers

- Quality – products and services must meet the customers' requirements

- Management – quality is actively managed rather than controlled so that problems are prevented from occurring.

TQM Priniples

- **Get it right, first time**
  Costs of prevention are less than the costs of correction; achieve zero rejects and 100% quality

- **Continuous improvement**
  A zero defect goal may not be obtainable. It does however provide a target

- **Customer focus**
  Quality is examined from a customer perspective, aimed at meeting customer needs and expectations.

Conformance costs:	Non-conformance costs:
Appraisal costs	Internal failure costs
Prevention costs	External failure costs

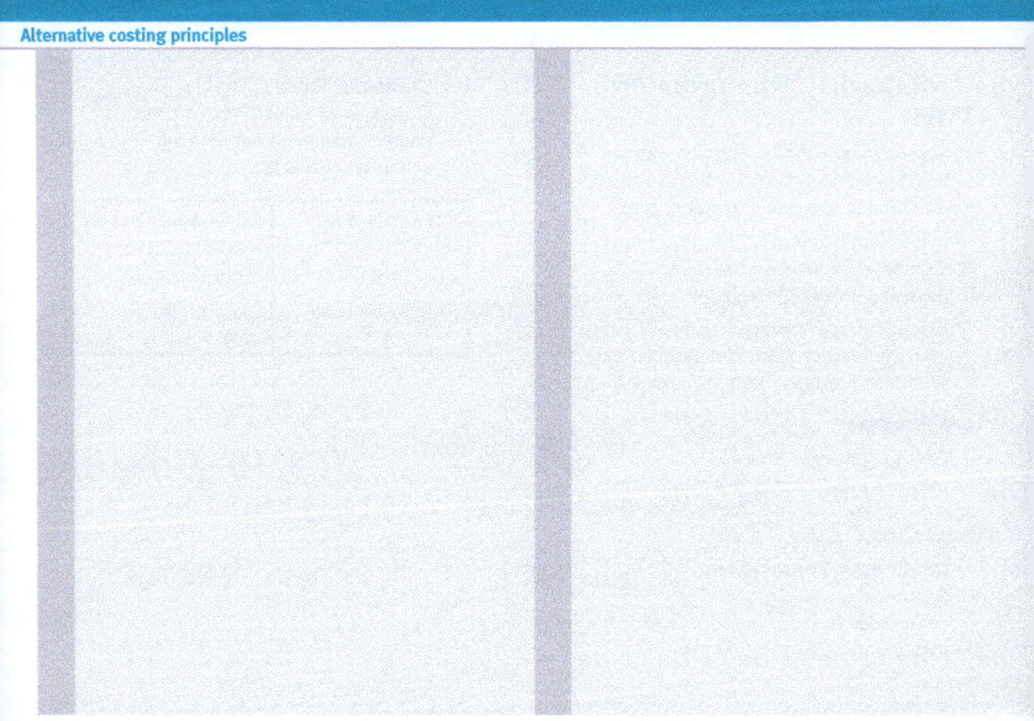

Statistical techniques

In this chapter

- Regression analysis.
- Time series analysis.
- Index numbers.

You will be given the formulae for regression analysis however it is important that you also understand the significance of each of the variables used and the meaning of r and r^2. You will need to know how to smooth out actual data to give a trend line using time series analysis (moving averages) and also how to adjust data using index numbers.

Regression analysis

Regression

Given 2 variables, x (independent variable), and y (dependent variable), least squares regression is a way of finding the line of best fit through the scatter diagram.

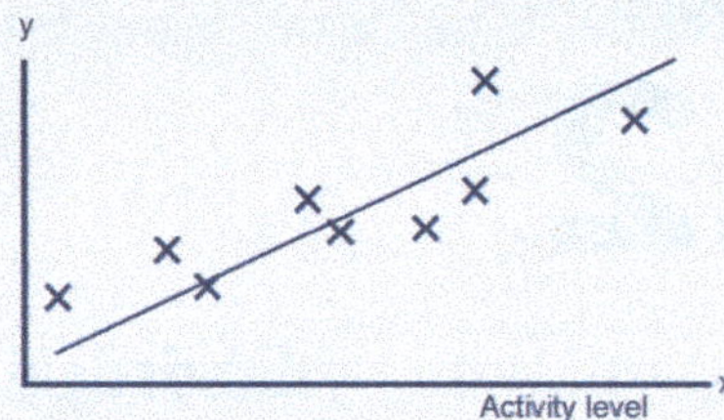

The equation of the line of best fit is:

$$y = a + bx$$

where a is the y value when x is 0, and b is the change in y when x increases by one unit.

In the context of cost estimation:

y represents the total cost

x represents the production volume in units

a represents the total fixed cost

b represents the variable cost per unit.

To find a and b, use the following formulae (both given):

$$b = \frac{n\sum xy - \sum x \sum y}{n\sum x^2 - (\sum x)^2} \quad \text{and} \quad a = \frac{\sum y}{n} - b\frac{\sum x}{n}$$

Correlation coefficient (r)

Definition

r measures the strength of a linear relationship between 2 variables.

- The **correlation coefficient** can only take values between -1 and +1

- A value of +1 indicates perfect positive correlation

- A value of 0 indicates no correlation

- A value of -1 indicates perfect negative correlation.

- A high correlation coefficient does not prove a causal relationship.

To find r (formula given)

$$r = \frac{n\sum xy - \sum x \sum y}{\sqrt{[n\sum x^2 - (\sum x)^2]\,[n\sum y^2 - (\sum y)^2]}}$$

Coefficient of determination (r^2)

Definition

r^2 is the square of the correlation coefficient. It shows how much of the variation in the dependent variable is explained by the variation in the independent variable.

The rest of the variation is due to:

- random fluctutations, or

- other specific factors not identified.

Note: 'spurious correlation' can occur when there appears to be correlation but the changes in both sets of figures are due to a third factor.

Example

If r = 0.95, r^2 = 0.90 or 90%

This means that 90% of the variation in the dependent variable is explained by the variation in the independent variable.

Time series analysis

Time series analysis is a term used to describe techniques for analysing a time series, in order to:

- identify whether there is any underlying historical trend and if there is, measure it

- use this analysis of the historical trend to forecast the trend into the future

- identify whether there are any seasonal variations around the trend, and if there is measure them

- apply estimated seasonal variations to a trend line forecast in order to prepare a forecast season by season.

A time series has 4 components:

- **Trend** – upwards, downwards or sideways.

- **Seasonal variations** – short term fluctuations in value due to different circumstances which occur at different times of the year, on different days of the week, different times of day.

- **Cyclical variations** – medium term to long term influences usually associated with the economy. These cycles are rarely of consistent length. Cyclical variations are often associated with the economy.

- **Residual or random variations** – is a difference caused by irregular items, which could not be predicted.

Moving averages

A moving average is a series of averages calculated from time series data. It is a technique used to smooth out the peaks and troughs in the data.

Index numbers

An index number is a technique for comparing, over time, changes in some feature of a group of items (e.g. price, quantity consumed, etc) by expressing the property each year as a percentage of some earlier year. The calculation is:

Current period index/base year index x 100

Types of index numbers

- A **simple** index is one that measures the changes in either price or quantity of a single item.

- A **chain base** index number expresses each year's value as a percentage of the value for the previous year.

- A **weighted** index measures the change in overall price or overall quantity of a number of different items compared to the base year.

Budgeting

In this chapter

- The purpose of budgets.

- Preparing budgets.

- Motivation.

- Incentive schemes.

- Participative budgeting.

- Functional budgets.

- Cash budgets.

- What if analysis.

- Scenario planning.

- Budgetary control cycle.

- Fixed, flexible and flexed budgets.

- Responsibility accounting.

- Controllable and uncontrollable costs.

For the exam you need to understand why budgets are prepared and calculate simple budgets for the various inputs to production. You also need to be able to work with simple flexible and flexed budgets; for this a steady, systematic approach is important.

The purpose of budgets

A budget is a quantitative expression of a plan of action prepared in advance of the period to which it relates.

- Budgets set out the costs and revenues that are expected to be incurred or earned in future periods.

Preparing budgets

Stages in budget preparation

Define long term objectives of the business

↓

Form budget committee to communicate budget policy, set and approve budgets.

Budget committee often includes:

- Chief executive
- Budget officer (management accountant)
- Departmental or functional heads

↓

Produce budget manual.

- Instructions on preparing and using budgets
- Details of responsibilities – including organisation chart and list of budget holders

↓

Identify principal budget factor – the limiting factor which limits the activity of the organisation.

- Usually sales but could be a scarce resource

↓

Produce budget for principal budget factor

↓

Produce and approve other budgets based on budget for limiting factor

↓

Review actual results and compare with budget to calculate variances

Different types of budget

Definition

The master budget includes the budgeted statement of profit or loss, the cash budget and budgeted statement of financial position (balance sheet).

Definition

A continuous budget is a budget which is prepared a year (or budget period) ahead and is updated regularly by adding a further accounting period (month, quarter) when the first accounting period has expired. Continuous budgets are also known as rolling budgets.

Motivation

Motivation is the drive or urge to achieve an end result. An individual is motivated if they are moving forward to achieving goals or objectives.

There is evidence which suggests that management accounting planning and control systems can have a significant effect on manager and employee motivation.

These include:

- the level at which budgets and performance targets are set

- manager and employee reward systems

- the extent to which employees participate in the budget setting process.

Budgets should provide a challenge for employees and managers that is achievable with an appropriate level of effort. The right level of difficulty is that which is acceptable to that individual manager. This level of acceptability will differ from manager to manager, as each individual behaves and reacts in a different way in similar circumstances.

Incentive schemes

Budgets by themselves have a limited motivational effect. It is the reward structure that is linked to achieving the budget requirements, or lack of reward for non-achievement, which provides the real underlying motivational potential of budgets.

Characteristics of a good employee reward system are as follows:

- Fairness
- Motivational
- Understandable
- Consistently applied
- Objective
- Universal

There are three main types of incentive schemes

- Performance related pay (PRP)
- Bonus schemes
- Profit sharing

Participative budgeting

The **top down** approach is where budgets are set by higher levels of management and then communicated to the lower levels of management to whose areas of responsibility they relate. This is also known as an imposed budget.

The **bottom up** approach to budgeting is where lower level managers are involved in setting budget targets. This is known as a participative budget.

Functional budgets

Definition

A functional budget is a budget of income and/or expenditure which applies to a particular function. The main **functional budgets** that you need to be able to prepare are as follows:

- sales budget

- production budget

- raw material usage budget

- raw material purchases budget

- labour budget

- overheads budget.

Sales budget (principal budget factor)		Sales revenue for each product for the period **Sales budget = expected number of units x planned selling price**
Production budget		Production levels for product to enable budgeted sales volumes **Budgeted production = forecast sales + closing inventory of finished goods – opening inventory of finished goods**
Material budgets	Usage budget	Material required to produce production levels. Usually expressed as quantity of each material required. **Material usage budget = budgeted production for each product x quantity of material required to produce one unit**
	Purchases budget	Amount of material which needs to be purchased to meet production budget. Usually expressed as quantity and value of material to be purchased. **Material purchases budget = material usage budget + closing inventory – opening inventory**
Labour budget		Cost of labour required to produce budgeted production levels **Labour budget = number of hours required for the production x labour rate per hour**

Overhead budget		Overhead costs to produce budgeted production levels **Budgeted level of activity x standard overhead rate** Where relevant activity is based on activity over which overheads are apportioned e.g. machine hours to produce budgeted production x production overheads per machine hour

Example

	Product A	Product B
Planned sales	100 units	200 units
Selling price	$40	$30
Opening inventory	12 units	20 units
Labour hours per unit	2 hours	1 hour
Machine hours per unit	1 hour	3 hours

Materials required:

	Material X	Material Y
Opening inventory of raw materials	36kg	44kg
Requirement per unit of product A	2kg	3kg
Requirement per unit of product B	2kg	1kg
Purchase price per kg	$0.50	$1.00

The company plans to halve all inventory levels over the period.

Labour rate per hour = $10

Variable overhead rate = $1.50 per machine hour

Fixed overhead rate = $0.50 per machine hour

Sales budget (principal budget factor)		Product A	Product B	Total
	Sales units	**100**	**200**	300 units
	Sales revenue	100 x 40 = $4,000	200 x $30 = $6,000	$10,000

Production budget		Product A	Product B
	Sales (units)	100	200
	Closing inventory (units)	6	10
	Opening inventory (units)	(12)	(20)
	Budgeted production (units)	**94**	**190**

Material budgets	Usage budget		Material X (kg)	Material Y (kg)
		Required for product A	94 x 2 = 188	94 x 3 = 282
		Required for product B	190 x 2 = 380	190 x 1 = 190
		Total	**568**	**472**
	Purchases budget		Material X	Material Y
		Usage budget (kg)	568	472
	Purchases budget		Material X	Material Y
		Usage budget (kg)	568	472
		Closing inventory (units)	18	22
		Opening inventory (units)	(36)	(44)
		Materials purchases budget (units)		
			550	450
		Materials purchases budget ($)	**$275**	**$450**
		Total materials purchases budget = $450 + $275 = $725		

Labour budget	Hours required for product A	94 x 2 = 188 hours
	Hours required for product B	190 x 1 = 190 hours
	Total hours required	378 hours
	Total labour budget	**$3,780**
Overhead budget	Machine hrs required for product A	94 x 1 = 94 hours
	Machine hrs required for product B	190 x 3 = 570 hours
	Total machine hours required	**664** hours
	Variable overhead budget	664 x 1.50 = $996
	Fixed overhead budget	664 x 0.50 = $332
	Total overhead budget	**$1,328**

Cash budgets

A **cash forecast** is an estimate of cash receipts and payments for a future period under existing conditions.

A **cash budget** is a commitment to a plan for cash receipts and payments for a future period after taking any action necessary to bring the forecast into line with the overall business plan.

Cash forecasts and budgets consider cash flows – so be careful to make sure that the transactions you are calculating involve **only cash items**.

Proforma for a cash budget

	July £	Aug £	Sept £
RECEIPTS			
Cash sales			
Cash from receivables			
Capital introduced			
Total receipts			
PAYMENTS			
Expenses			
Payments to payables			
Purchases of non-current assets			
Total payments			
Net cash flow			
Opening bank balance			
Closing bank balance			

Example of cash receipts from receivables

The forecast sales for an organisation are as follows:

Sales	January	February	March	April
	$	$	$	$
Sales	6,000	8,000	4,000	5,000

All sales are on credit and receivables tend to pay in the following pattern:

	%
In month of sale	10
In month after sale	40
Two months after sale	45

The organisation expects the rate of irrecoverable debts to be 5%.

Calculate the forecast cash receipts from receivables in April.

Cash from:	$
April sales: 10% × $5,000	500
March sales: 40% × $4,000	1,600
February sales: 45% × $8,000	3,600
	5,700

Example of cash payment to payables

A manufacturing business makes and sells widgets. Each widget requires two units of raw materials, which cost $3 each. The business will take one month's credit.

Production quantities of widgets each month are as follows:

Month	Units
December	50,000
January	55,000
February	60,000
March	65,000

Calculate the payment to be made in April.

Quantity of raw material purchased:

Material (@ 2 units per widget)

	Production	December	January	February	March
	Units	Units	Units	Units	Units
December	50,000	100,000			
January	55,000		110,000		
February	60,000			120,000	
March	65,000				130,000
		———	———	———	———
Total purchases		100,000	110,000	120,000	130,000
		———	———	———	———
At $3 per unit		300,000	330,000	360,000	390,000

	January	February	March
	$	$	$
Payment to suppliers	300,000	330,000	360,000

At the end of March, there will be payables of $390,000 for raw materials purchased, which will be paid in April.

What if analysis

'What if' analysis is a form of sensitivity analysis that allows:

- the effects of changes in one or more data value to be quickly recalculated

- budgets to be amended/adjusted easily.

Spreadsheets are very useful in what if analysis.

Scenario planning

Scenario planning has proved a very useful tool in forecasting, strategic planning and business modelling.

Budgetary control cycle

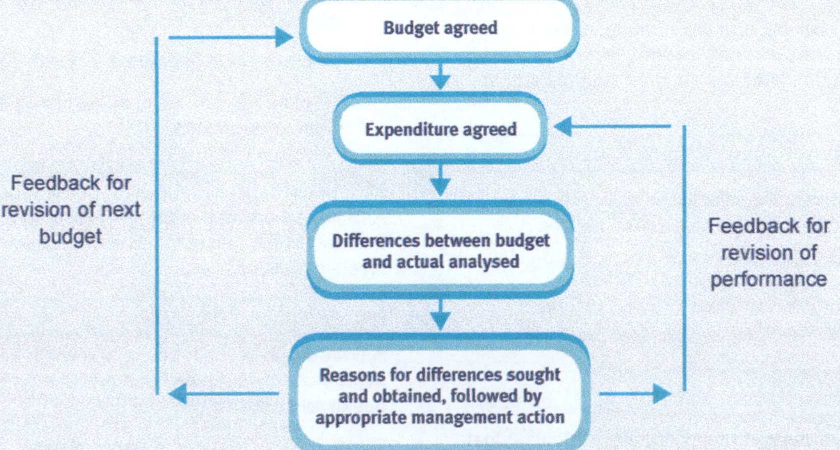

Feedback is the comparison of budget and actual performance with a view to revising plans, budgets or operations. The control action takes place after the event.

Planning is a form of **feedforward** control.

Fixed, flexible and flexed budgets

Fixed, flexible and flexed budgets are used within the budgetary control cycle where the planned budget is compared with the actual results.

Definition

Variances are differences arising between the original budget and actual results.

Adverse variances (Adv, A) decrease profits.

Favourable variances (Fav, F) increase profits

Definition

A **fixed budget** compares the original budget with the actual results.

However fixed budgets:

- remain unchanged even though the volume of activity changes

- therefore, do not compare like with like

- therefore, do not assist in identifying the cause of variances.

Definition

A **flexible budget** is a budget prepared at the start of the period for different possible levels of activity

Definition

A **flexed budget** changes as the volume of activity changes. Flexed budgets are more useful for budgetary control purposes.

To produce a flexible and flexed budget:

- it is necessary to identify the cost behaviour of the different items in the original budget

- it may be necessary to use the high/low method to separate the fixed and variable elements of semi-variable costs.

Flexed budgets and budget variances

The overall differences between the original budget and actual results are total budget variances.

The total variance can be analysed into volume and expenditure variances:

- volume variance: shows the difference in costs due to the change in actual activity from budget. It is the difference between the fixed (original) and flexed budget

- expenditure variance: shows the difference in costs due to the actual expenditure differing from the fixed budget figures. It is the difference between the flexed budget and the actual results.

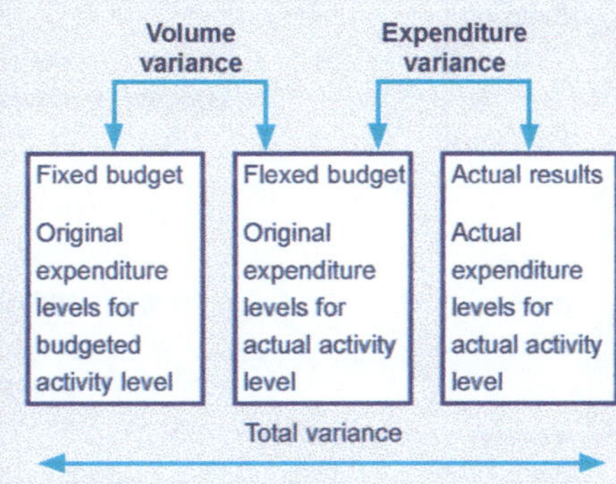

Example

	Fixed budget	Volume variance	Flexed budget	Expenditure variance	Actual results	Total variance
Production (units)	1000	200	800		800	
	$	$	$	$	$	$
Direct materials	500	**100 (F)**	400	**(125) (A)**	525	**(25) (A)**
Direct labour	2000	**400 (F)**	1600	**250 (F)**	1350	**650 (F)**
Variable production overhead	1000	**200 (F)**	800	**(75) (A)**	875	**125 (F)**
Fixed production overhead	400		400	**(25) (A)**	425	**(25) (A)**
Total	3900	**700 (F)**	3200	**25 (F)**	3175	**725 (F)**

Note: To convert from fixed budget to flexed budget, all estimates of variable cost expenditure are flexed with respect to output (800/1000). Fixed costs are not flexed with respect to output because they are fixed and do not depend on output volumes.

Responsibility accounting

Budgetary control and responsibility accounting are seen to be inseparable.

It is important to ensure that each manager has a well defined area of responsibility and the authority to make decisions within that area, and that no parts of the organisation remain as 'grey' areas where it is uncertain who is responsible for them. If this is put into effect properly, each area of the organisation's activities is the responsibility of a manager. This structure should then be reflected in the organisation chart.

An area of responsibility may be structured as:

- a cost centre – where the manager is responsible for cost control only

- a revenue centre – where the manager is responsible for generation of revenues only

- a profit centre – the manager has control over sales revenues as well as costs

- an investment centre – the manager is empowered to take decisions about capital investment for his department.

Each centre has its own budget, and the manager receives control information relevant to that budget centre. Costs (and possibly revenue, assets and liabilities) must be traced to the person primarily responsible for taking the related decisions, and identified with the appropriate department.

Controllable and uncontrollable costs

Controllable costs and revenues are those costs and revenues which result from decisions within the authority of a particular manager or unit within the organisation. These should be used to assess the performance of managers.

The aim under a responsibility accounting system will be to assign and report on the cost to the person having primary responsibility.

14

Capital budgeting

In this chapter

- Types of interest.
- Payback period.
- Net present value.
- Internal rate of return (IRR).
- Annuities.
- Perpetuities.

This chapter contains 3 main techniques for appraisal of capital investments. You need to know the calculations and the theory behind each technique.

Non-relevant cost terminology

- Sunk costs
- Committed costs
- Noncash flow costs
- General fixed overheads

Types of interest

Simple interest is calculated based on the original sum invested. Any interest earned in earlier periods is not included. Simple interest is often used for a single investment period that is less than a year.

Compound interest calculates the future (or terminal value) of a given sum invested today for a number of years.

The **nominal interest rate** is the stated interest rate for a time period – for example a month or a year.

The **effective interest rate** is the interest rate that includes the effects of compounding a nominal interest rate.

Payback period

The payback period is the time a project will take to pay back the money spent on it. It is based on expected cash flows and provides a measure of liquidity. This is the time which elapses until the invested capital is recovered. It considers cash flows only. It can be calculated with and without discounted cash flows.

- Compare the payback period to the company's maximum return time allowed and if the payback is quicker the project should be accepted.

- Faced with mutually exclusive projects choose the project with the quickest payback.

	Payback Period	
Year	Cash flow $000	Cumulative cash flow $000
0	(450)	(450)
1	200	(250)
2	150	(100)
3	50	(50)
4	100	50
5	120	

Payback period = 3 years and 50/100 × 12 months

= 3 years and 6 months

	Discounted Payback period			
Year	Cash flow $000	Discount factor	Discounted cash flow $000	Cumulative discounted cash flow
0	(450)		(450)	(450)
1	200	0.909	182	(268)
2	150	0.826	124	(144)
3	50	0.751	38	(106)
4	100	0.683	68	(38)
5	120	0.621	75	37

Discounted payback period = 4 years and 38/75 × 12 months

= 4 years and 6 months

Advantages	Disadvantages
• Simple to understand • A project with a long payback period tends to be riskier than one with a short payback period. • Payback is a simple measure of Risk • Uses cash flows, not subjective accounting profits • Emphasises the cash flows in the earlier years • Firms selecting projects on the basis of payback periods may avoid liquidity problems	• Is not a measure of absolute profitability • Ignores the time value of money Note: A discounted payback period may be calculated to overcome this problem • Does not take into account cash flows beyond the payback period

Net present value

The NPV represents the surplus funds (after funding the investment) earned on the project. This means that it tells us the impact on shareholder wealth. The net benefit or loss of benefit in present value terms from an investment opportunity.

- Any project with a positive NPV is viable.

- Projects with a negative NPV are not viable.

- Faced with mutually exclusive projects, choose the project with the highest NPV.

Example

Mickey Ltd is considering two mutually exclusive projects with the following details:

Project A

Initial investment $450,000

Scrap value in year 5 $20,000

Year:	1	2	3	4	5
Annual cash flows ($000)	200	150	100	100	100

Project B

Initial investment $100,000
Scrap value in year 5 $10,000

Year:	1	2	3	4	5
Annual cash flows ($000)	50	40	30	20	20

Assume that the initial investment is at the start of the project and the annual cash flows are at the end of each year.

Required:

Calculate the Net Present Value for Projects A and B if the relevant cost of capital is 10%. Calculate which project has the highest NPV.

	Project A			Project B	
Year	Discount factor	Cash flow	Present value	Cash flow	Present value
		$000	$000	$000	$000
0		(450)	(450)	(100)	(100)
1	0.909	200	181.8	50	45.45
2	0.826	150	123.9	40	33.04
3	0.751	100	75.1	30	22.53
4	0.683	100	68.3	20	13.66
5	0.621	120	74.52	30	18.63
		NPV	= 73.62	NPV	= 33.31

Advantages	Disadvantages
• Does consider the time value of money • It is a measure of absolute Profitability • Considers cash flows • It considers the whole life of the Project • A company selecting projects on the basis of NPV maximisation should maximise shareholders	• Fairly complex • Not well understood by nonfinancial managers • It may be difficult to determine the cost of capital

Internal rate of return (IRR)

This is the rate of return, or discount rate, at which the project has a NPV of zero.

- If the IRR is greater than the cost of capital the project should be accepted.
- Faced with mutually exclusive projects choose the project with the higher IRR.

Technique:

(1) Calculate two NPVs for the project at two different costs of capital

(2) Use the following formula to find the IRR:

$$IRR = L + \frac{NL}{NL - NH} \times (H - L)$$

where:

L = Lower rate of interest

H = Higher rate of interest

NL = NPV at lower rate of interest

NH = NPV at higher rate of interest.

Example

Calculate the internal rate of return.

At 20% the NPV is $8,510

At 30% the NPV is – $9,150

$$IRR = 20 + \frac{8,510}{8,510 - -9,150} \times (30 - 20)$$

IRR = 24.8%

Advantages	Disadvantages
<ul><li>Does consider the time value of money</li><li>As a percentage return it is easily understood by nonfinancial managers</li><li>Considers cash flows</li><li>It considers the whole life of the project</li><li>It can be calculated without reference to the cost of capital</li><li>A company selecting projects where the IRR exceeds the cost of capital should increase shareholders' wealth</li></ul>	<ul><li>It is not a measure of absolute profitability</li><li>Interpolation only provides an estimate of the true IRR</li><li>Fairly complicated to calculate – although spreadsheets now have built in programs</li><li>The IRR of projects may conflict with the NPV. If this occurs the NPV must take precedence</li></ul>

Annuities

An annuity is a constant annual cash flow for a number of years.

The formula is:

$$AF = \frac{1 - (1+r)^{-n}}{r}$$

Perpetuities

A perpetuity is an annual cash flow that occurs forever.

The formula is:

$$PV = \frac{\text{Cash flow}}{r}$$

or

$$PV = \text{cash flow} \times \frac{1}{r}$$

15

Standard costing

In this chapter

- The purpose of standard costing.

- Advantages and disadvantages of standard costing.

- Types of standard.

- Variance calculations.

- The causes of variances.

- Operating statements.

This is a very popular topic for multiple-choice questions! Learn the techniques so you can calculate the variances quickly and accurately.

Don't rely on common sense with fixed overhead variances under absorption costing – learn it!

One way that the examiner can easily test your understanding of variances is to ask you to calculate the following instead of straightforward variance calculations:

- actual figures from variances and standards

- standards from variances and actual figures.

The purpose of standard costing

Standard costing helps management control the business:

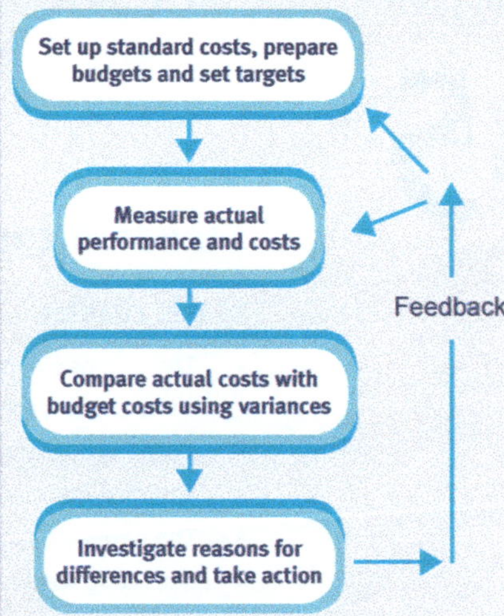

Standard costs are normally collected on a standard cost card.

- They may be based on absorption costing or marginal costing (variable cost only).

Advantages and disadvantages of standard costing

Advantages	Disadvantages
• Detailed examination of the organisation when standards are being set • Comparison of actual cost to standard cost for performance evaluation • Facilitates management by exception by concentrating on investigation of most significant variances • Simplifies bookkeeping and inventory records where all inventory is valued at standard	• Standards can quickly become out of date • Establishing standards, monitoring the system and investigating variances is costly • Unrealistic standards can demotivate staff

Types of standard

Ideal	Attainable
What would be expected under perfect operating conditions	What would be expected under normal operating conditions
Basic	**Current**
A standard left unchanged from period to period	A standard adjusted for specific issues relating to the current period

Variance calculations

Points to remember

There are two areas where the variance calculations depends on whether you are working with a marginal or an absorption costing systems:

- the sales volume variance

- fixed overhead variances.

	Marginal costing	Absorption costing
Sales volume variance	• Calculated using the standard contribution per unit	• Calculated using the standard profit per unit
	Note – The standard selling price is not used because when volumes change so do production costs and the purpose of the variance is to show the impact on profit or contribution	

Fixed overhead variances	Marginal costing	Absorption costing
	• Marginal costing does not relate fixed overheads to cost units	• Fixed overheads are related to cost units by using absorption rates.
	• There is no under- or over-absorption, and the fixed overhead incurred is as shown in the statement of profit or loss as a period cost	• The fixed overhead total variance is equivalent to the under- or over - absorption of overhead in a period.
	• There is therefore no fixed overhead volume variance. The fixed overhead expenditure variance is the difference between actual expenditure and budgeted expenditure and is the total variance.	• The fixed overhead volume variance can be further subdivided into capacity and efficiency variance.

Calculating variances

SALES VARIANCES

Sales volume variance

Absorption costing

(Budgeted quantity sold – actual quantity sold) x standard profit per unit

Marginal costing

(Budgeted quantity sold – actual quantity sold) x standard contribution per unit

Sales price variance

(Budgeted sales price – actual sales price) x actual quantity sold

---

Example

JDC operates a standard cost accounting system. The following information has been extracted from its standard cost card and budgets:

Budgeted sales volume	5,000 units
Budgeted selling price	$10.00 per unit
Standard variable cost	$5.60 per unit
Standard total cost	$7.50 per unit

JDC's actual sales were 4,500 units at a selling price of $12.00. What is the sales volume variance and the sales price variance under marginal and absorption costing?

Solution

Standard contribution/unit = $10 – $5.60 = $4.40.

Sales volume variance under marginal costing = (Actual sales – Budgeted sales) x Standard contribution per unit = (4,500 – 5,000) x $4.40 = $2,200 (A).

Standard profit/unit = $10 – $7.50 = $2.50

Sales volume variance under absorption costing = (actual sales – Budgeted sales) × Standard profit per unit = (4,500 - 5,000) × $2.50 = $1,250 (A)

Sales price variance under marginal and absorption costing = (Actual sales price – budgeted sales prices) × Actual quantity = ($12 – $10) × 4,500 = $9,000 (F)

DIRECT MATERIALS VARIANCES

Actual quantity x	Actual Price	} Price Variance
Actual quantity x	Standard Price	
Standard quantity	x Standard Price	} Usage Variance

(flexed to Actual Production)

Example

Company A uses 6kg of Material M in its unique product P. Each kg of M costs £5. In January, 6,500kg of M were used to produce 1,000 units of P, at a cost of £39,000.

Calculate :

(i)   the material price variance,
(ii) the material usage variance.

Solution

(i)

Actual Quantity x Actual Price
  6,500 kgs   x   £6.00 = £39,000

Actual Quantity x Standard Price
  6,500 kgs   x   £5.00 = £32,500

Material price variance   = £6,500 A

The price variance is adverse for Material M, the standard material cost was lower than actual material costs.

(ii)

Actual Quantity x Standard Price

   6,500 kgs   x £5.00   =   £32,500

Standard Quantity x Standard Price

   6,000 kgs   x £5.00   =   £30,000

Material usage variance   =   **£2,500 A**

The usage variance is adverse, so actual materials used were more than the standard quantity.

DIRECT LABOUR VARIANCES

Actual hours x   Actual Rate   **Rate**

Actual hours x   Standard   **Variance**
                 Rate

Standard   x   Standard   **Efficiency**

hours   Rate   **Variance**

(flexed to Actual Production)

Example

The standard direct labour cost of Product H is $21 per unit, and each unit is expected to take 3.5 hours to make. The budget was to produce 22,000 units, but in the period, only 21,000 units were actually made. The time required to produce these units was 75,000 hours, which had a labour cost of $431,250. What was the direct labour rate variance and the direct labour efficiency variance in the period?

Solution

Actual hours   × Actual rate
75,000   = $431,250

                               Rate variance = $18,750 (F)

Actual hours   × Standard rate
75,000 $21/3.50   = $450,000

                             Efficiency variance = $9,000 (A)

Standard hours   × Standard rate
21,000 × 3.5 $21/3.50   = $441,000

VARIABLE OVERHEADS VARIANCES

Actual hours x   Actual Rate   } **Expenditure Variance**

Actual hours x   Standard Rate

Standard hours x   Standard Rate   } **Efficiency Variance**

(flexed to Actual Production)

FIXED OVERHEADS VARIANCES

Absorption costing

Actual expenditure

Expenditure variance

Budgeted expenditure

Volume variance

Actual units produced x fixed overhead absorption rate per unit

or, splitting down the volume variance into capacity and efficiency variances:

Actual expenditure

Expenditure variance

Budgeted expenditure

Capacity variance

Actual hours x fixed overhead absorption rate per hour

Efficiency variance

Standard hours for actual production x fixed overhead absorption rate per hour

Example

A company operates a standard absorption costing system. The standard fixed production overhead rate is $15 per hour.

The following data relate to last month :

Actual hours worked	5,500
Budgeted hours	5,000
Standard hours for actual production	4,800

Calculate :

(i) the fixed production overhead capacity variance

(ii) the fixed production overhead efficiency variance

Solution

(i) Capacity variance (5,000 – 5,500) hours at $15 per hour = $7,500 F

Note that working more hours than budgeted produces a favourable fixed overhead capacity variance.

This is because working more hours does not cause more fixed overhead expenditure, but does make better use of the fixed resources.

(ii) Efficiency variance

Standard hours for actual production 4,800 x OAR $15	=	$72,000
Less Actual hours 5,500 x OAR $15	=	$82,500
Efficiency variance	=	$10,500 A

The causes of variances

Variance	Possible causes
Sales volume variance	• Price change • Change in size of market • Change in market share – competition
Sales price variance	• Deliberate – e.g. drop price to boost sales • Due to change in quality? • Competition
Materials price variance	• Change in supplier • Different material bought • Efforts of purchasing department • Commodity price changes
Materials usage variance	• Different materials (link to price?) • Different machinery • Efforts of production department • Change in mix of materials?

Labour price (or rate) variance	<ul><li>Productivity link</li><li>Strikes</li><li>Different grade of labour</li></ul>
Labour efficiency variance	<ul><li>Link to rate?</li><li>Change in quality of materials</li><li>Change in machinery</li><li>Efforts of production department</li></ul>
Variable O/H expenditure (or rate) variance	<ul><li>Machines wearing out?</li><li>Machines overworked due to increase in production volume</li></ul>
Variable O/H efficiency variance	<ul><li>Same as for labour efficiency variance</li></ul>
Fixed O/H expenditure variance	<ul><li>Change in rent, etc</li></ul>

Operating statements

Variances are summarised in an operating statement. The main differences between absorption and marginal costing operating statements are as follows:

- the marginal costing operating statement has a sales volume variance that is calculated using the standard contribution per unit (rather than a standard profit per unit as in absorption costing)

- there is no fixed overhead volume variance in a marginal costing system.

Operating statements – total absorption costing

Variances are often summarised in an operating statement (or reconciliation statement).

Absorption costing operating statement			$
Budgeted profit			
Sales volume variance (using profit per unit)			——
Standard profit on actual sales			
Sales price variance			
Cost variances:	F $	A $	
Material price			
Material usage			
Labour rate			
Labour efficiency			
Variable overhead rate			
Variable overhead efficiency			
Fixed overhead volume – Production			
Fixed overhead expenditure – Production			
Fixed overhead expenditure – Non-Production	——	——	
Total			——
Actual profit			——
(Note the bold highlights the differences from the marginal costing version.)			

Marginal costing operating statement			$
Budgeted contribution			
Sales volume variance (using contribution per unit)			———
Standard contribution on actual sales			
Sales price variance			———
Cost variances:			
	F	A	
	$	$	
Material price			
Material usage			
Labour rate			
Labour efficiency			
Variable overhead rate			
Variable overhead efficiency			
Actual contribution			
Budgeted fixed on			
Fixed overhead expenditure – Production			
Fixed overhead expenditure – Non-Production	———	———	
Total			———
Actual profit			———

Note

There is no fixed overhead volume variance (and therefore capacity and efficiency variances) in a marginal costing operating statement.

16

Performance measurement techniques

In this chapter

- Financial performance measurement.
- Divisional performance.
- Non-financial performance measurement.
- The Balanced Scorecard.
- Benchmarking.
- Manufacturing industries.
- Non-profit and public sector.

Exam focus

This chapter contains the formulae for the performance indicators that you are likely to come across.

You need to make sure you use the right ones in the right situations so make sure you read the scenarios/questions carefully.

Financial performance measurement

Profitability

Return on capital employed (ROCE) = operating profit ÷ (noncurrent liabilities + total equity) %

Return on sales (ROS) = operating profit ÷ revenue %

Gross margin = gross profit ÷ revenue %

Asset turnover = revenue ÷ capital employed

Liquidity

Current ratio = current assets ÷ current liabilities

Quick ratio = (current assets − inventory) ÷ current liabilities

Activity

Inventory days = inventory ÷ cost of sales × 365

Receivable days = receivables ÷ credit sales × 365

Payable days = payables ÷ credit purchases × 365

Risk

Capital gearing = noncurrent liabilities (debt) ÷ ordinary shareholders funds (equity) %

or

Capital gearing = noncurrent liabilities (debt) ÷ (noncurrent liabilities + ordinary shareholders funds (debt + equity)) %

Interest cover = operating profit ÷ finance cost.

Divisional Performance

Measurement of divisional performance needs to be based on controllable costs and controllable revenue therefore controllable profits.

Two calculations that can be used to measure divisional performance are return on investment and residual income.

$$ROI = \frac{\text{Controllable profit}}{\text{Controllable capital employed}} \times 100$$

RI = Controllable profit − Notional interest on capital

Non-financial performance measurement

Examples of non-financial indicators:

- Competitiveness
- Resource utilisation
- Quality of service
- Customer satisfaction
- Quality of working
- Innovation
- Responsiveness (lead time)
- Quality of output
- Flexibility (ability to react to changing demand and a changing environment)

Productivity measures

Production/volume ratio

$$\frac{\text{Actual output measured in standard hours}}{\text{Budgeted production hours}} \times 100$$

Capacity ratio

$$\frac{\text{Actual production hours worked}}{\text{Budgeted production hours}} \times 100$$

Efficiency ratio

$$\frac{\text{Actual output measured in standard hours}}{\text{Actual production hours worked}} \times 100$$

The Balanced Scorecard

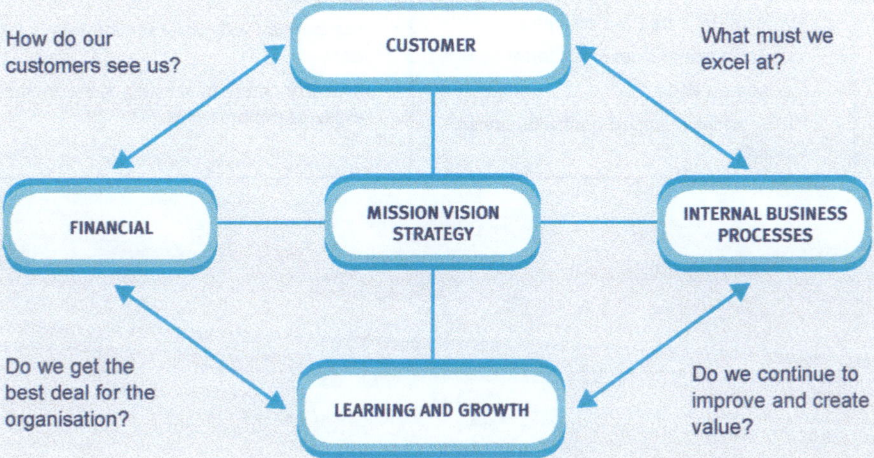

Advantages	Disadvantages
• uses four perspectives less able to distort the performance measure • harder to hide bad performance • long term rather than short term • focuses on KPIs • KPIs can be changed as the business changes	• large numbers of calculations required • subjective • comparison with other businesses is not easy • arbitrary nature of arriving at the overall index of performance

Benchmarking

Benchmarking is the management process which involves comparison of competences with best practice including comparison beyond the organisation's own industry. There are several types of benchmarking including:

- Internal benchmarks – comparisons between different departments or functions within an organisation.

- Competitive benchmarks – comparisons with competitors in the business sector – through inter-firm comparison schemes.

- Functional benchmarks – comparisons with organisations with similar core activities that are not a competitor.

- Strategic benchmarks – comparisons of market share and profit margins.

Manufacturing industries

Cost control is vital for manufacturing industries.

Contract costing

Specific for large scale contracting operations you can calculate the attributable profit part way through a long term contract:

$$\frac{\text{Value of work certified to date}}{\text{Contract price}} \times \text{Overall expected profit}$$

OR

$$\frac{\text{Costs incurred to date}}{\text{Total expected costs to completion}} \times \text{Overall expected profit}$$

Job costing

For job costing is it important to look at the type of firm as this will influence the type of measure used:

- Practising accountants – ratio of chargeable time to total time
- Garages – average age of inventories of spares
- Printers – cost per printed page
- Tree surgeons – tipping time to chipping time

Batch costing

As with job costing, batch costing should consider the type of firm to decide on the type of measure to be used:

- Clothing manufacturers – quantity of material loss
- Furniture manufacturers – levels of inventories held
- Bakers – baking time to oven heating time
- Electrical goods makers – number of quality control failures

Process costing

Appropriate measures include:

- Clothing manufacturers – quantity of material loss
- Furniture manufacturers – levels of inventories held
- Bakers – baking time to oven heating time
- Electrical goods makers – number of quality control failures

Service quality

Quality is seen to be a particularly important nonfinancial performance indicator in the service sector. Quality can be measured by:

- customer surveys
- management inspections
- fault monitoring

Non-profit and public sector

There are said to be two main problems involved in assessing performance of these organisations:

- the problem of identifying and measuring objectives

- the problem of identifying and measuring outputs.

Value for money (VFM)

VFM concept revolves around the 3Es, as follows:

- Economy (an input measure) – measures the relationship between money spent and the inputs. Are the resources used the cheapest possible for the quality required?

$$\frac{\text{Standard input}}{\text{Actual input}} \times 100$$

- Efficiency (link inputs with outputs) – is the maximum output being achieved from the resources used?

$$\frac{\text{Actual output}}{\text{Actual input}} \times 100$$

- Effectiveness (links outputs with objectives) – to what extent to which the outputs generated achieve the objectives of the organisation

$$\frac{\text{Actual output}}{\text{Standard output}} \times 100$$

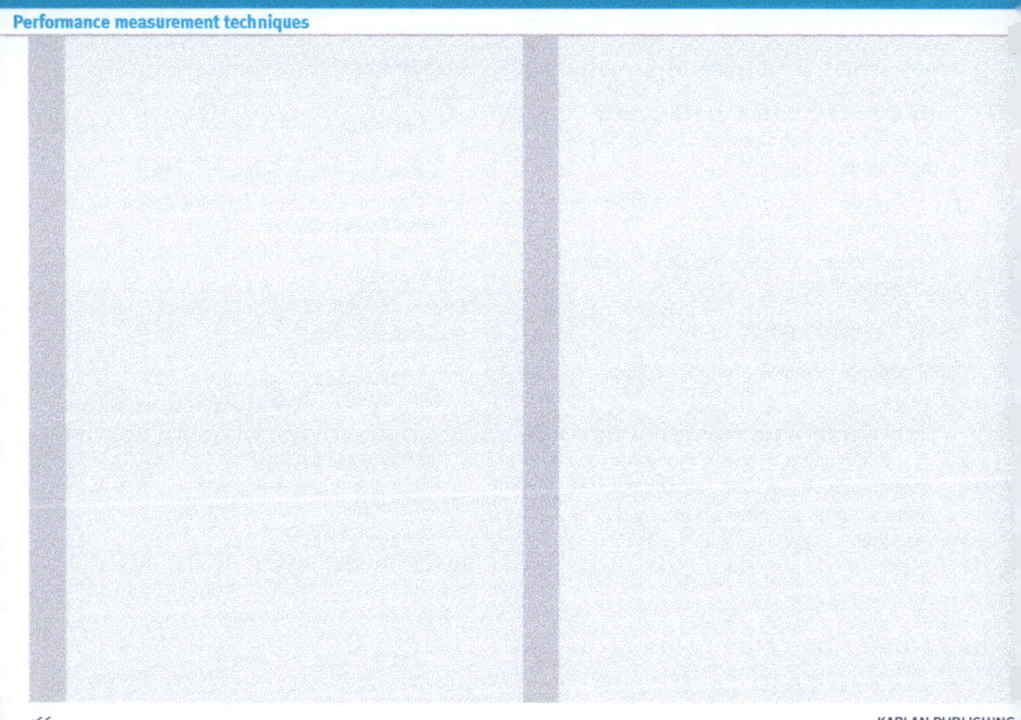

17

Spreadsheets

In this chapter

- Spreadsheets.
- Uses of spreadsheets.

You could be asked why spreadsheets are useful to a business. Equally you could be asked to combine your knowledge of spreadsheets with calculations in earlier chapters to produce formulae.

Spreadsheets

A spreadsheet is a computer package that is used to manipulate data.

To enter a formula

- select the cell where you want to enter the formula

- press the equal sign (=) on the keyboard (or click on the sign in the formula bar, if one is shown)

- key in the formula directly from the keyboard or use the mouse to select the cells you want in the formula. There are no spaces in a formula

- press the <Enter> key

- when you have entered a formula, the resulting value appears in that cell. The formula is only visible in the formula bar.

Uses of spreadsheets

Much of the data of a company is likely to be held on a number of spreadsheets. They are a convenient way of setting up all sorts of charts, records and tables, including:

Budgeting and forecasting

Preparing budgets and forecasts are classic applications of spreadsheets, as they allow estimates to be changed without having to recalculate everything manually, e.g. here is an extract from a cash flow forecast.

'What-if' analysis

- The power of spreadsheets is that the data held in any one cell can be made dependent on that held in other cells.

- This means that changing a value in one cell can set off a chain reaction of changes through other related cells.

chapter 17

- This allows 'what if?' analysis to be quickly and easily carried out, e.g. 'what if sales are 10% lower than expected?'

Reporting performance

Performance appraisal usually involves calculating ratios, possibly involving comparatives between companies and from one year to the next.

- A neat way of doing this is to input the raw data, such as financial statements on one sheet and calculate the ratios on another.

Variance analysis

Variance analysis involves management comparing actual results with budget and then investigating the differences.

Advantages of spreadsheets

Spreadsheets are designed to analyse data and sort list items, not for long term storage of raw data. A spreadsheet should be used for 'crunching' numbers and storage of single list items. Advantages of spreadsheets include the following:

- Spreadsheet programs are relatively easy to use.

- Little training is required to get started with using spreadsheets.

- Most data managers are familiar with spreadsheets.

- They also include graphing functions that allow for quick reporting and analysis of data. There is more on the graphics function of spreadsheets at the end of this section.

Disadvantages of spreadsheets

Disadvantages of spreadsheets include the following:

- Data must be recopied over and over again to maintain it in separate data files.

- Spreadsheets are not able to identify data errors efficiently.

- Spreadsheets lack detailed sorting and querying abilities.

- There can be sharing violations among users wishing to view or change data at the same time.

- Spreadsheets are restricted to a finite number of records, and can require a large amount of hard drive space for data storage.

Index

3Es 165
3Vs 13

A

Abnormal gain 77
Abnormal loss 76
Absorption 63
Absorption costing 60, 69
Absorption costing profit statement 71
Activity based costing 98
Allocation 60
Annuities 141
Apportionment 60
Average cost per unit 76
Average inventory 43

B

Balanced scorecard 161
Batch costing 75
Benchmarking 163
Big data 13
Bonus schemes 53
Budget 110

Budget committee 111
Budget preparation 111
Budgets 110
Budget variances 127
Buffer or safety stock 43
By-products 90

C

Capacity variance 151
Cash budget 121
Cash forecast 121
Cluster sampling 12
Coefficient of determination 105
Coefficient of variation 15
Common costs 90
Component bar chart 25
Compound bar chart 26
Conformance costs: 101
Continuous budget 112
Continuous stocktaking 46
Contract costing 163
Contribution 68
Control 3

Controllable costs 130
Conversion cost 92
Conversion costs 80
Correlation 105
Correlation coefficient 105
Cost accounting 7
Cost allocation 60
Cost cards 37
Cost centre 4, 5, 36
Cost driver 98
Cost equations 36
cost object 36
Cost pool 98
cost unit 36
Cost unit 36

D

Data 2
Decision making 3
Direct costs 33
Direct labour 51
Direct labour cost 51
Discounted Payback period 134

E

Economic batch quantity 45
Economic order quantity 44
Efficiency variance 151
Expected values 18
Expenditure variance 127, 151

F

FIFO 84
FIFO (first in, first out) 47
Financial accounting 7
Financial performance measurement 158
Fixed budget 126
Fixed cost 33
Fixed overhead expenditure , 147
Fixed overheads variances 151
Flexed budget 126
Flexible budget 126
Functional budget 114
Functional budgets 114

H

High-low method 34
Holding costs 42

I

Idle time 51
Incentive schemes 113
Index numbers 107
Indirect costs 33
Indirect expenses 60
Indirect labour 51
Indirect labour cost 51
Information 2
Interest 132
Internal rate of return 139
Internal sources 10
Investment centre 4, 5
IRR 139

J

Job costing 74
Joint costs 90
Joint products 90

L

Labour account 52
Labour budget 114, 115
Labour capacity ratio 55
Labour efficiency ratio 54
Labour production volume ratio 55
Labour turnover 54
Labour variances 150
Life cycle costing 99
LIFO (last in, first out) 47
Linear cost functions 36

M

Management accounting 7
Marginal cost 68
Marginal costing 69
Marginal costing profit statement 71
Master budget 112
Material price variance 149
Material purchases budget 114, 115
Materials inventory account 48
Material usage budget 114, 115
Material usage variance 150

Maximum inventory level 43
Mean 15
Median 15
Minimum inventory level 43
Mode 15
Motivation 112
Multiple line chart 26

N

Net present value 136
Non-conformance costs: 101
Non-production costs 30, 32
Non-relevant cost 132
Normal distribution 20
Normal loss 76
NPV 136

O

OAR 63
Operating statements 155
Operational 4
Ordering costs 42
Over-absorbed 63

Over-absorption 64
Overhead absorption rate (OAR) 63
Overhead budget 116
Overheads 60
Overtime premium 51

P

Participative budgeting 113
Payback period 133
Percentage component bar chart 25
Periodic stocktaking 46
Perpetual inventory 46
Perpetuities 141
Piecework schemes 53
Pie chart 27
Planning 3
Planning, decision making and control 2
Principal budget factor 111
Probability 18
Process account 79
Process costing 75
Production budget 115
Production costs 30, 31
Productivity measures 160

Product life cycle 100
Profit 68
Profit centre 4, 5

Q

Quota sampling 12

R

Range 15
Reapportionment 61
Regression analysis 104
Remuneration methods 53
Reorder levels 43
Responsibility accounting 129
Responsibility centres 4
Revenue centre 4, 5

S

Sales budget 115
Sales price variance 148
Sales variances 148
Sales volume variance 148
Sampling 11

Scenario planning 124
Semi-variable cost 34
Service cost analysis 95
Service cost units 94
Service industries 94
Service product costs 95
Service quality 164
Simple bar chart 24
Spreadsheets 168
Standard costing 144
Standard deviation 15
Standard hour 55
Standards 145
Stepped fixed cost 34
Stores ledger card 46
Strategic 4
Stratified sampling 11
Systematic sampling 11

T

Tactical 4
Target costing 99
Time based schemes 53
Time series analysis 106
Total Quality Management (TQM) 101

U

Uncontrollable costs 130
Under-absorbed 64
Under-absorption 64
Under- or over-absorption 69

V

Value analysis 99
Value engineering 99
Value for money 165
Variable cost 33
Variable overheads variances 151
Variance 15
Variance calculations 146
Variances 126
Volume variance 127, 151

W

Weighted average cost (AVCO) 47
Weighted average cost of production 81
What if analysis 124

Z

Z score 20